ACE
Short-Response
WRITING

15 Mini-Lessons, Strategies, and Scaffolds to Help Students Craft Meaningful Short Responses

BY GRACE LONG

■ SCHOLASTIC

New York • Toronto • London • Auckland • Sydney
Mexico City • New Delhi • Hong Kong • Buenos Aires

Dedication

*In loving memory of my mother, Angela. You loved unconditionally,
you saw the best in people, you were a model learner. I'm striving to be like you.*

This book is also dedicated to all the teachers and students who give endlessly.

Acknowledgments

I would like to express great appreciation to the countless individuals who have contributed to this book. Words cannot express my gratitude for those I've had the privilege to work with. To all fellow teachers, thank you for the sharing in the collaboration, conversation, and passion to always be thinking about next steps for students.

To all the students who have ever set foot in my classroom, thank you for allowing me to teach you, and thank you for allowing me to learn from you.

To Team Harvard, Cristal and Lorraine, our teamwork was life-changing for me as a teacher and, I believe, for our students. Thank you for showing me that with trust and true collaboration, amazing things can happen.

To UCLA Teacher Education Program, thank you for the commitment to social justice and for the constant reminder of why I became an educator.

To Lawndale Elementary School District, where I started my career as a teacher, thank you for the firm foundation in the journey of providing access and equity to all learners. Thank you for the many wonderful years of being a part of the LESD family.

To El Segundo Unified School District, thank you for providing the opportunity to take risks, stretch, and grow in unexpected ways. Thank you for leadership opportunities and allowing me to experience instructional impact from a totally different perspective.

To the Cotsen Foundation, thank you for being a critical component in my development as a teacher. Through your vision and support, I was blessed with a solid foundation and pedagogy to reach all learners by being artful in my approach.

To CoT, my teacher friends and family, thank you for the many laughs, meals, and support sessions. Thank you for the encouragement to write this book and for using ACE in your classrooms. Your talents and skills in writing and editing, art and graphic design, cooking and care-taking, and teaching made this possible.

To Scholastic, especially my editor, Maria Chang, thank you for believing in this book and taking it from hope to reality.

And to my family—Brandon, thank you for your love and support. Jadon, Corban, and Evangeline, you are my inspiration and bring more joy than words can describe.

....

Editor: Maria L. Chang | Cover design by Tannaz Fassihi | Interior design by Abby Dening
Photo ©: 105: wavebreakmedia/Shutterstock.

ISBN: 978-1-338-28560-4
Copyright © 2019 by Grace Long.
Text passages on pages 38, 133–138 © by Scholastic Inc.
All rights reserved. Printed in the U.S.A.
First printing, March 2019.

1 2 3 4 5 6 7 8 9 10   131   24 23 22 21 20 19

TABLE OF CONTENTS

INTRODUCTION

"I know what I want to say, I just don't know how to say it."
– JULIETTE, 6TH-GRADE STUDENT

As teachers, we serve students with various abilities and personalities. Our class population often includes students who struggle with academic performance as well as children who are gifted and high-achieving. We have English-language learners, students with diverse learning abilities, and scholars who may be intrinsically motivated. Some may be strong in one content area but weak in another. Through it all, we strive to differentiate to meet the unique needs of every child in our classroom.

As we continue to be reflective in our practice, we ask ourselves: *How do we attempt to meet the needs of all our students? How do we meet the rigorous demands of today's higher standards? How do we help our students get ready for college and careers?* With so much to do in so little time, we constantly look for instructional strategies that will make the most impact and yield the most benefit to our students.

Although we may not believe in a "one size fits all" approach to teaching, we do need to be selective about utilizing instructional strategies that would help advance all our students. The philosophy behind the ACE strategy is that all our students are capable thinkers, and it is our job as teachers to provide them with a structure and a system for thinking that would be useful to them. **ACE stems from the belief that students know much more than they think they do; they just need to learn how to express their knowledge effectively.** As they learn how to do so, they empower themselves as learners and thinkers.

What Is ACE?

"ACE" is the nickname we use for the structure and strategies presented in this book. ACE is an acronym for:

> **A** = Answer the question
> **C** = Cite evidence
> **E** = Elaborate your thinking

ACE is much more than an acronym, however. The ACE strategy is a pathway to critical thinking. It's about eliciting the critical thinking skills that our students already have in order to succeed in any given context. It's about providing a safe structure for students to validate what they are already thinking.

After many years in the classroom, I've started to see similar patterns of responses from students.

- I've seen the "lost in translation" response. Students sound very articulate and verbose when called on in class, but somehow when it comes to putting their ideas on paper, their thoughts seem to get lost in translation. What they say orally looks nothing like what they write on paper.

- Another familiar type of written response is the "run-on." These start off as great ideas, but the writing goes on and on. And although there are plenty of words written on the page, I'm often left confused about what point students were trying to make.

- I've also gotten the "blank" response. This is when there is absolutely nothing on their paper—students get stuck tapping their pencils or thinking about what to write. This type of response, or lack thereof, usually comes from students who struggle with confidence and feel the need to "get it right." Although they have plenty of content knowledge, experiences, and thoughts, they are unsure about using them in an academic setting.

- Finally, I often encounter the "one-word" response. I might ask thought-provoking questions during instruction, expecting a deep, thoughtful response, only to get literally one word on the paper.

When I asked my students why they continually turn in responses that do not exemplify their knowledge and capabilities, I would hear comments like Juliette's: "I know what I want to say, I just don't know how to say it." This confirmed the need to provide a pathway to support my students' thinking. It's not that they don't know the answer; they just don't know how to express it. They need a starting point—a structure or framework—to elicit their knowledge. My students need tools to access the knowledge they already have. It was no longer about getting the knowledge in, but rather a matter of how to pull the knowledge out.

This is what *ACE Short-Response Writing* is all about. It is designed to support the diverse needs of students, using the knowledge they already have. This is growth mindset in action. As my students became more and more comfortable with using the ACE strategy, their confidence grew as thinkers. They went from scribbling rambling paragraphs to composing cohesive, clear paragraphs; from giving blank stares to being engaged and on task; from jotting one-word answers to penning elaborate responses.

In the context of school, ACE is especially helpful anytime students have to make a claim and justify their position. This includes the areas of reading comprehension, informative writing, argumentative essay writing, deep thinking, and conversation. As you and your students grow accustomed to using the ACE strategy, it will become very evident that this strategy also can draw out critical thinking in other content areas, such as math, science, history, and art.

At first, the ACE strategy may seem formulaic. However, the intention is to provide students structure in order to build their confidence in using the tool. Once they gain confidence (and it takes only a few lessons), students' creativity is unlocked and their responses become far from formulaic, especially when elaborating upon their thoughts. No matter their ability level, students are able to access ACE and make it as simple as they need it to be, or as complicated and deep as they are capable of.

The following are simple examples of ACE responses from the classroom.

ACE IN CLASSROOM DISCUSSION

Question: What is a personality trait that you would use to describe Mrs. Moore?

Answer: Mrs. Moore is a funny teacher.

Cite evidence: Even in the middle of a math lesson, she'll crack a joke.

Elaborate: This is significant because when students laugh and learn at the same time, the lesson is more memorable.

ACE IN LITERARY RESPONSE

Q: How would you describe the character Despereaux from *The Tale of Despereaux* (by Kate DiCamillo)?

A: Despereaux can be considered a brave character.

C: On page 56, the Mouse Council gives him a chance to avoid the dungeon if he renounces the princess, but he refuses to do so.

E: This shows he is brave, because many people would have succumbed to peer pressure. But Despereaux sticks to what his own heart believes and does what he thinks is right, despite the consequences.

ACE IN HISTORY

Q: When studying the Ancient Greeks, do you believe the Spartans or Athenians were the more powerful city-state?

A: I believe the Spartans were the more powerful city-state.

C: The Spartan males started military school at the age of 6 and continued into their 60s (evidence from textbook).

E: This is significant because in ancient times, invaders were always trying to conquer new lands. A culture of physically strong boys and men is more prepared to win wars and defeat invaders.

ACE IN MATH

Q: There is an equal number of children and dogs. There are 60 legs altogether. How many children and dogs are there?

A: There are 10 children and 10 dogs.

C: 10 children have 20 legs, and 10 dogs have 40 legs. 20 + 40 = 60 legs

E: To find the answer, I thought about the fact that dogs have two times as many legs as children. Knowing that there are the same number of children and dogs also helped. So I used the "guess and check" strategy until I came up with 10 children and 10 dogs.

ACE IN SCIENCE

Q: What is at the base of the ocean food web?

A: Phytoplankton are at the base of the ocean food web.

C: These tiny organisms, which live near the ocean's surface, make their own food using the sun's energy.

E: This is significant because phytoplankton are food for zooplankton, which in turn are food for small fish and other ocean animals. These small animals, in turn, are eaten by larger animals, and so on. Without phytoplankton, the ocean food web would collapse, and most ocean animals would die out.

As you can see, the ACE strategy can be applied in many areas outside of English language arts. As you and your students become familiar with the strategy, opportunities to use it will become apparent. Students will ask, "Can I ACE this?" And you'll respond, "Of course!"

How Do We Teach ACE?

When beginning to teach students how to ACE their responses, focus on the structure and process rather than just the acronym. Students will pick up the acronym quite quickly, but we need to emphasize that the strategy is much more than just letters.

Begin by introducing the overall structure of ACE—the purpose, the process, and why it's important for students to respond in this way (Lesson 1). Continue to familiarize students with the ACE structure by pointing out instances when they can use ACE in classroom activities. These might include class discussions, open-ended questions, warm-ups, exit slips, and so on. Providing students with a variety of sentence starters for each component of ACE will help them become more comfortable with using this strategy (Lesson 2). Once you have introduced the overall structure, deepen students' understanding by explicitly teaching how to do each component of answering the question (Lesson 3), citing evidence (Lesson 4), and elaborating (Lessons 5 to 12).

You'll find that when students master the ACE structure, one-word answers decrease significantly. While this is a good first step, we are still looking to develop critical thinking skills. This is why teaching students the ACE structure is just the beginning.

How Does ACE Lead to Critical Thinking?

The National Council for Excellence in Critical Thinking (1987) defined *critical thinking* as "the intellectually disciplined process of actively and skillfully conceptualizing, applying, analyzing, synthesizing, and evaluating information" to reach an answer or conclusion.

With the ACE strategy, students are actively evaluating as they answer (A) a question or make a claim. They are analyzing and applying when they cite evidence (C) to support their claim. Finally, they are synthesizing and applying when they learn how to elaborate (E) their thinking.

The elaboration strategies are at the heart of ACE. This component is where students initially struggle the most, but it is also where they will shine the most. This is where their creativity and individuality are honored. We value students' interests, personalities, and experiences, and they can bring those to the table when making an argument. Students engage in thoughts such as, "How can I explain this? What can I pull from my bank of knowledge to prove my point? How do I make others see my point of view?" As students think about their thinking, they synthesize previous knowledge with a new purpose—these are critical thinking skills that all students need to learn in order to succeed in any college or career.

In Part II of this book, the series of lessons explicitly teach these eight elaboration strategies.

1. Explain Why
2. Cause and Effect
3. Compare and Contrast
4. Real-World Connection
5. Before and After
6. Show Your Voice
7. Say More
8. Visualize It

Since the ultimate hope is that students will use these lines of thinking beyond our classroom walls, teaching them how to use ACE to write paragraphs and essays (Lesson 13) and to respond to standardized tests (Lessons 14 and 15) solidifies how they can apply their thinking skills.

PART I
Implementation and Practice

These days, class assignments commonly ask students to make claims, cite evidence, and elaborate in their writing. But that is often the problem—students are given these assignments, but not necessarily taught how to do them. The lessons in this book address the issue of how to teach kids to **answer**, **cite evidence**, and uniquely, how to **elaborate**. Using acronyms, such as ACE, and coined phrases, such as the "Cause and Effect strategy," ensures these learned strategies stick. Naming the strategy provides a tangible tool students can pull out and use when needed.

The lessons in this book include a teacher version and a student version. The teacher version offers a script you can use (in *italics*) as a guideline for teaching the lesson. The purpose and context of each lesson is stated at the beginning, while notes and tips are embedded throughout the lesson. The teacher version also provides sample responses to the student activities. The reproducible student pages, called "Review & Practice," include a summary of the same lesson along with activities for partner and independent practice. Photocopy these pages and use them as handouts or activity sheets that students can insert into their writer's notebook for reference. You can also use Review & Practice as a model to create your own questions and assignments based on current subject matter in class.

Each lesson follows the same format. This explicit and predictable structure helps students know what to expect from each lesson. Each lesson includes:

Teaching Point This statement sets the expectation for the lesson. I find it very helpful to chart the date with the teaching point of the day. This serves as a good reference point for lessons taught and can often make conferencing with students more efficient. It speaks to the expectation that even though students learned something one day, they are expected to use that strategy from that day forward—not a one and done! For clarity, the teaching point is at the top of every lesson to remind both teachers and students of the purpose of the lesson and activity.

Connect This serves as the link or glue to other lessons and learning activities you've been doing in class. It provides a context for the lesson, putting students in a frame of mind to learn the new strategy.

Teach This portion of the lesson includes two very important components:

- **How Do I Do This?**—simple steps that guide students in applying the strategy

- **Teacher Model**—a clear example of the strategy in action

Having their own copy of these step-by-step directions and teacher model (included in their Review & Practice handouts) helps students when they go back and try the lesson on their own. They can also use these as a reference for future writing assignments. I've seen many instances when my students were able to "reteach" themselves because they had a copy of these in their writer's notebook.

In addition, conferencing becomes faster and more efficient because students have specific steps and language to use. Instead of "I need help with this," they will say, "I understand Steps 1 and 2, but I need help with Step 3." Or, "I have my claim down, but I'm not sure if this elaboration strategy matches my evidence." This gives you a quick way to see and compliment what they are doing well, and then move forward in the conferencing.

Partner Practice Working with a partner provides a safe space for students to try the new strategy. It offers opportunities for student talk, collaboration, and peer accountability. Giving students a chance to work together when learning something new often builds confidence, leading to the next stage of trying the concept on their own. Sample responses are provided and underlined.

Now You Try! After students have learned the lesson, seen the teacher model, understood the teaching point and expectations, and practiced and discussed the steps with a partner, they can try the strategy on their own. (This section also provides sample student responses, which are underlined.) As students work independently, you can conference with individuals.

Share and Reflect Conclude the lesson with this optional yet strategic student reflection activity. During this valuable extension, students practice critical thinking by sharing their responses and actively listening to their peers. For example, a classmate may have used a strategy in a way other students hadn't thought of before. Encourage students to write their reflections using the sentence starter or frame provided.

BETTER, NOT MORE

As you and your students grow more accustomed to using the ACE strategy, opportunities to apply them will become apparent. I know you don't need to add something else to your already full plate. Using the same content you currently teach in your classroom, you can simply tweak assignments to incorporate ACE as a way to frame the thinking in the work.

Here are a few more tips for helping students ACE their responses.

Name It – One of the key components of this book is the "official naming of things." It is much more efficient and effective when students remember the name of a strategy—such as Flip It, Lift the Line, or Cause and Effect—rather than all the questions or sentence starters associated with it. Continually refer to the strategies by name, as students will feel confident about "knowing that one." Staying consistent with the names of strategies also saves the trouble of having to ask numerous questions or requests. For example, instead of saying, "Don't forget to turn the question into a statement," you can simply say, "Flip It," and students will know what that means.

Use Highlighters – I recommend using colored highlighters to help students internalize the strategy. Have students use a green highlighter for their answer (A), yellow for citing evidence (C), and pink for elaboration (E). Stick to these three colors and use them consistently. Visuals and colors are helpful for all students, but especially for those who need more supports (e.g., language learners, students with exceptional needs).

Charts and Cards – In the appendix, you'll find reproducible charts for reference. You can display enlarged versions on the board or hand out copies to students to add to their writer's notebook. You can also use them to create the following:

- ACE Anchor Charts – With the help of students, make ACE posters with sentence starters and names of strategies to solidify the concepts and make the learning "official."
- ACE Cards – Have students make ACE cards to keep readily available on their desks for reference and quick starts.
- Elaboration Anchor Charts – Enlist students' help to create an anchor chart for each elaboration strategy, complete with a brief description and sentence starters.

LESSON 1
Introducing ACE

TEACHING POINT
Critical thinkers know how to ACE a question.

MATERIALS
- Review & Practice handout (pages 18–19)
- index cards
- green, yellow, pink highlighters (optional)*

This lesson introduces the overall structure of ACE. Students will see the value of using ACE in their response rather than just giving a one-word answer.

Formative Assessment Activity (optional): Before you begin the lesson, hand each student an index card. On the board, write: *What do you think is the most exciting sport?* Don't provide too much direction, such as asking them to write their answer in a complete sentence or giving them examples. Just see how they respond. I predict most students will give you a one-word answer, such as "basketball" or "soccer." Have students show their index cards so you can get a glimpse of how many wrote just one word. Some answers may be a complete sentence, but you most likely won't see too many paragraphs. Acknowledge their responses and ask students to put their index cards aside for now.

---

* Note: You may want to simultaneously introduce the use of three different-color highlighters with this strategy. Have students use the green highlighter for their answer (A), yellow for citing evidence (C), and pink for elaboration (E).

Continue with the lesson. At the end of the lesson, have students respond to the same question using the ACE structure. They should be impressed by their own pre- and post-ACE response.

Connect

Say to students: *Thinkers, we've been working hard to learn how to become successful scholars. Scholars are deep thinkers who make valid arguments. In schools these days, it is no longer enough just to give the correct answer. It is more important to think about how we can justify our answers and what evidence we have that our answers are correct. How do we know what we know? This is really deep thinking. Today, I want to show you a strategy that will begin to lead us to greater success as students and thinkers.*

Imagine that a teacher just gave a test. Student #1 says, "I BOMBED this test." Student #2 exclaims, "Wow! I ACE'd it!" What can we infer? Did both students feel good about how they did on the test? (No) What did the student mean when he said he ACE'd it? Was the test easy or difficult for this student? (Easy) Did the student feel confident or not confident about his performance on the test? (Confident) This is exactly what I want for you as scholars—I want you to ACE every question! And I don't just mean getting an A, but I also mean feeling confident that you did your best and that it was easy for you to answer the question.

Teach

Say to students: *Today I'm going to teach you a strategy for responding to questions. This strategy is called ACE. As you learn how to ACE your responses, I hope you will see that you actually know so much more than you might think! Anytime you encounter an open-ended question in which you are asked to provide evidence to support your thinking, I want you to ACE your response.*

Refer to the Teaching Point: "Critical thinkers know how to ACE a question." Then write the following on the board:

> ## WHAT IS ACE?
>
> **A** = Answer the question
>
> **C** = Cite evidence
>
> **E** = Elaborate your thinking

Critical thinkers don't just give an answer; they ACE it. When responding to a question, you want to sound as academic as possible. ACE'ing your answers will provide you with a structure to formulate your answers and responses. No more one-word answers!

HOW DO I DO THIS?

1. Read the question carefully.

2. Pause and think about what the question is really asking you.

3. Answer the question in a complete sentence.
   - *I think . . .*

4. Cite evidence about the topic that supports your answer.
   - *One reason . . .*

5. Elaborate by saying how your evidence proves your answer.
   - *This is significant because . . .*

TEACHER MODEL

Now, watch me as I ACE a question. The first step is to read the question carefully.

Question: What animal do you consider fascinating?

First, let me think about what the question is really asking me. Is it asking me what is my favorite animal? (No) Is it asking me what animals do I see at the zoo? (No) The question is asking what animal do I consider fascinating. Wow! There are so many animals I could talk about—cheetahs, snakes, kangaroos—but I want to focus on one that I consider particularly fascinating. I've got one! I think camels are fascinating animals. I'm going to record my **answer** *now.*

Answer: I think camels are fascinating animals.

Now I want to **cite evidence** *that will support my thinking. I need to ask myself, "Why are camels fascinating? What's my reason for thinking this?" I know from my schema—things I already know or have seen—that camels can go without water for a few months. I definitely want to use that as my evidence.*

Cite evidence: One reason is that camels can go without water for up to seven months under extreme conditions.

The next thing I need to do is **elaborate**. *One way I can elaborate on my evidence is by explaining how this evidence proves my answer. I need to ask myself, "So what? How does this prove my answer?" Well, this is significant because humans can't last nowhere near as long without water. Let me write this down.*

Elaborate: This is significant because humans can last only three to five days without water.

I want to make sure that I've ACE'd the question, so let's reread my response. (Reread the question and the responses together.) *Fabulous! I used today's teaching strategy to help me answer the question completely and thoughtfully.*

Partner Practice

Distribute copies of the Review & Practice handout. Then pair up students and say: *Now, I'd like you to try the ACE strategy with a partner. Here is a new question for you to answer:* Which sport do you think relies on teamwork the most to win a game?

Remember to practice the steps from "How Do I Do This?" Think about the question and then **answer** *it using a complete sentence. Use your schema—what you already know or have seen—to help you* **cite evidence.** *Finally,* **elaborate** *by explaining how your evidence helps prove your answer. Partner A, you ask the question. Partner B, talk through your ACE response using the sentence starters provided. Then switch roles.*

Allow time for students to work with their partner to complete the activity. As they work, circulate around the room and keep an eye out for outstanding examples of today's teaching point.

SAMPLE RESPONSE

Q: Which sport do you think relies on teamwork the most to win a game?

A: I think basketball relies on teamwork the most to win a game.

C: One reason is that there are different positions in the game, such as center, small forward, power forward, shooting guard, and point guard.

E: This is significant because each player relies on other players to do their part so they can shoot the ball in the basket.

Allow time for a peer share. Say: *I think we are ready to share. As I walked around the room, I heard several students who were able to ACE the question. Let's hear a few responses.* Call on student volunteers to share their responses.

Then say: *You guys did a great job! I think you're ready to do this on your own. Here are more questions for you to use as practice. Be sure to use today's strategy to help you record your answer.*

Now You Try!

Have students answer the questions in their Review & Practice handout, using ACE to help them articulate their answers. Students may write their responses either on the handout or in their writer's notebook.

Note: You may see a lot of repetition in student responses for A and E. This is to be expected for the beginning ACE lessons and will be addressed when we discuss Elaboration strategies in later lessons. Remember, the goal of this lesson is simply to get students used to the three components of the ACE structure. We will teach them how to use critical thinking and go deeper into their thought process in upcoming lessons.

SAMPLE RESPONSES

1) What habit do you think is most important for a successful student?

A: I think <u>the most important habit for a successful student is to pay attention in class.</u>

C: One reason <u>is that a student who pays attention will more likely remember information when he or she needs to take a test.</u>

E: This is significant because <u>not only does the student show the teacher he or she cares about learning, but his or her grades will be higher as well.</u>

2) What invention do you think is most valuable to people today?

A: I think <u>the most valuable invention today is the cell phone.</u>

C: One reason <u>is that people can get in touch with each other no matter where they are.</u>

E: This is significant because <u>it allows parents and their children to be in contact with each other at all times.</u>

Share and Reflect

If you did the pre-formative assessment, have students go back to their original response on their index cards. Ask them to rewrite their response on the back of the card, this time using the ACE format. Invite a few students to share their before and after responses. Remind the class to listen carefully while others are sharing. Afterwards, have students write a response using this frame:

- *I heard _____ say . . .*
- *This made me realize _____.*

Ask students how many think their ACE response is better than their first attempt. Point out that they didn't actually learn any new knowledge about their sport, but that they had this ACE response in them all along. Using the ACE strategy simply provided them with a structure to express their thinking.

LESSON 1
INTRODUCING ACE

Name: _____ Date: _____

TEACHING POINT
Critical thinkers know how to ACE a question.

What Is ACE?

A = Answer the question

C = Cite evidence

E = Elaborate your thinking

How Do I Do This?

1. Read the question carefully.

2. Pause and think about what the question is really asking you.

3. Answer the question in a complete sentence.
- *I think . . .*

4. Cite evidence about the topic that supports your answer.
- *One reason . . .*

5. Elaborate by saying how your evidence proves your answer.
- *This is significant because . . .*

Teacher Model

Q: What animal do you consider fascinating?

A: I think camels are fascinating animals.

C: One reason is that camels can go without water for up to seven months under extreme conditions.

E: This is significant because humans can last only three to five days without water.

Partner Practice

Work with your partner to ACE the question below.

Question: Which sport do you think relies on teamwork the most to win a game?

A: I think _____

_____

C: One reason _____

_____

E: This is significant because _____

_____

Now You Try!

Use today's teaching point to ACE the questions below.

1) What habit do you think is most important for a successful student?

A: I think _____

_____

C: One reason _____

_____

E: This is significant because _____

_____

2) What invention do you think is most valuable to people today?

A: I think _____

_____

C: One reason _____

_____

E: This is significant because _____

_____

LESSON 2
Using Sentence Starters

MATERIALS

- Review & Practice handout (pages 25–26)
- green, yellow, pink highlighters (optional)

Now that students are acquainted with the ACE strategy, this lesson offers more sentence starters they can use to respond to questions. These sentence starters help scaffold and prompt student thinking.

Connect

Say to students: *Thinkers, we have pushed ourselves as scholars. We know that ACE is a strategy to help strengthen, develop, and show our thinking. No matter where we are—whether at school or at home—we want to be able to express our point of view clearly. We want to ACE our responses by providing evidence to support our answer and elaborating thoughtfully.*

Did you know that this is what lawyers do for a living? When working on a case, lawyers take a position and provide evidence to convince people to see things their way and to prove their point. They also elaborate to explain how the evidence supports their position on the case.

As you learn more about the ACE strategy, think of yourselves as lawyers. Lawyers know that there are multiple ways to prove their point. Today we are going to add on to ways we can ACE our responses.

Teach

Say to students: *Let's review what we already know from the previous ACE lesson.* (If necessary, refer to the Review & Practice handout from the previous lesson.)

> ### REVIEW OF ACE
>
> **A** = Answer the question *("I think . . .")*
>
> **C** = Cite evidence *("One reason . . .")*
>
> **E** = Elaborate your thinking *("This is significant because . . .")*

Tell students: *We want to gain more experience with using ACE. That means we need new strategies to practice. Let's see how.*

On the board, draw the three-column chart below. Under each heading, write only the first sentence starter, which are from the previous lesson. Say: *Now, I'm going to show you other sentence starters to prompt our thinking.* Add the new sentence starters under each column.

Answer the question	Cite evidence	Elaborate your thinking
• *I think . . .* • *I believe . . .* • *People should/should not . . .*	• *One reason . . .* • *For example . . .* • *In my school/home/ personal experience . . .*	• *This is significant because . . .* • *This shows . . .* • *Many people ___, but . . .* • *One effect of ___ would be . . .*

HOW DO I DO THIS?

1. Read the question carefully and think about the topic.

2. Get ready to ACE your thinking. Select a sentence starter from each column.

3. Reread the question and your response.

4. Ask yourself the following:
   - *Did I answer the question in a complete sentence?*
   - *Did I select evidence that supports my thinking?*
   - *Did I elaborate on my thinking?*

5. If you answered "yes" to these questions, then you've ACE'd your response!

TEACHER MODEL

We don't want to be like a musician who performs the same old song every time. We want to be able to use a variety of sentence starters and not always rely on the same language. Watch as I use these new sentence starters. Let's take a look at a new question.

Q: What is one way we can help the environment?

I want to think carefully about what the question is asking and about the topic. I know that there are many ways to help our environment. For example, we could reduce our trash and recycle and compost more. I'm going to pick a new sentence starter to use for my **answer***. I'll start with "I believe . . ."*

A: I believe one way we can help the environment is to reduce trash by recycling and composting more.

Now I want to **cite evidence** *to support my thinking. In this case, evidence can be from my schema, or things I already know or have seen. I actually don't have far to look—I throw out the trash at home every night, and it's a lot! But since we started recycling and composting, the amount of trash we throw out has become a lot less. I want to use this as my evidence. Let me think of another sentence starter to use. I'll begin my evidence with "For example . . ."*

C: For example, my family used to throw out a huge amount of trash each day, but since we started recycling and composting, we have less trash.

The next thing I need to do is **elaborate***. I want to say more about the evidence I chose as important. I need to ask myself, "How does this evidence prove that reducing trash helps our environment?" Hmm . . . Well, it means less waste ends up in landfills or gets into our oceans. Let me write this down.*

E: One effect of recycling and composting would be less solid waste ending up in landfills and polluting our waters.

I want to make sure that I've ACE'd the question, so let's reread my response. (Reread the question and the responses together.) Fabulous! I expanded my ACE'ing by using some new sentence starters to help me answer the question completely and thoughtfully.

Partner Practice

Distribute copies of the Review & Practice handout. Then pair up students and say: *Now I'd like you to try one together. Here is a new question for you to answer:* What can people do to stop bullying?

    Remember to use a variety of sentence starters to ACE your question. Focus on the topic, and then answer the question using a complete sentence. Use your schema to help you cite evidence. Finally, elaborate to explain how your evidence helps prove your answer.

    Allow time for students to work with their partner to complete the activity. As they work, circulate around the room, keeping an eye out for outstanding examples of today's teaching point. Afterwards, invite students to share their responses with the class.

SAMPLE RESPONSE

Q: What can people do to stop bullying?

A: <u>People can stop being bystanders when they witness bullying.</u>

C: <u>In my school experience, I've actually seen bullying stop when another kid stepped up and said something to the bully.</u>

E: <u>Many people would just stand there and be passive bystanders, but I think we should be advocates. Don't just stand there; say something, do something!*</u>

    Tell students: *Now I'd like you to reread your ACE response. Did you answer the question in a complete sentence? Did you select evidence that supports your thinking? Did you elaborate on your thinking? Raise your hand if you were able to answer "yes" to all of these questions. Congratulations! You've ACE'd today's lesson by using a variety of sentence starters to show your thinking. I think you're ready to do this on your own. Here are more questions for you to use as practice. Be sure to use a variety of sentence starters to help you ACE your thinking.*

Now You Try!

Have students answer the questions on their Review & Practice handout, using a variety of ACE sentence starters to help them develop and articulate their answers. Students may write their responses either on the handout or in their writer's notebook.

---

* Note: This is the Compare and Contrast Elaboration strategy, which is the focus of Lesson 7. For now, just provide the sentence starters as a way to prompt thinking.

SAMPLE RESPONSES

1) What quality do you think is most important in a friend?

A: I think the most important quality in a friend is trustworthiness.

C: For example, if you tell your friend something you don't want other people to know, you want to feel secure knowing that your secret is safe with your friend.

E: This is significant because oftentimes friendships end when one person becomes a victim of gossip and other people talk about that person when it is none of their business.

2) Should students be allowed to use their personal devices during school?

A: I believe students should be allowed to use their personal devices during school.

C: One reason is that computers, smartphones, tablets, and other electronic devices can be a quick and efficient way to get information.

E: One effect of having easy access to electronics is that we could have endless resources on the internet for research papers.

Share and Reflect

Ask students to do a quick write about why using a variety of sentence starters to ACE is an important thinking strategy. Then invite them to share their responses with the class. Remind students to listen as others share. Afterwards, ask them to write a response using this sentence frame:

- *I heard _____ say . . .*
- *This made me realize _____.*

LESSON 2
USING SENTENCE STARTERS

Name: _____ Date: _____

TEACHING POINT
Critical thinkers can use variety of sentence starters to ACE a question.

How Do I Do This?

1. Read the question carefully and think about the topic.

2. Get ready to ACE your thinking. Select a sentence starter from each column.

3. Reread the question and your response.

4. Ask yourself the following:

   • Did I answer the question in a complete sentence?

   • Did I select evidence that supports my thinking?

   • Did I elaborate on my thinking?

5. If you answered "yes" to the above questions, then you've ACE'd your response!

What sentence starters can we use?

Answer the question	Cite evidence	Elaborate your thinking
• *I think . . .* • *I believe . . .* • *People should/should not . . .*	• *One reason . . .* • *For example . . .* • *From my school/home/ personal experience . . .*	• *This is significant because . . .* • *This shows . . .* • *Many people ___, but . . .* • *One effect of ___ would be . . .*

Teacher Model

Q: What is one way we can help the environment?

A: I believe one way we can help the environment is to reduce trash by recycling and composting more.

C: For example, my family used to throw out a huge amount of trash each day, but since we started recycling and composting, we have less trash.

E: One effect of recycling and composting would be less solid waste ending up in landfills and polluting our waters.

Partner Practice

Turn and talk with your partner about this question. What do you have in your schema that might help you ACE this question?

Q: What can people do to stop bullying?

A: _____

_____

C: _____

_____

E: _____

_____

Now You Try!

Use a variety of sentence starters to ACE the questions below.

1) What quality do you think is most important in a friend?

A: _____

_____

C: _____

_____

E: _____

_____

2) Should students be allowed to use their personal devices during school?

A: _____

_____

C: _____

_____

E: _____

_____

LESSON 3
Answer Using the "Flip It" Strategy

TEACHING POINT

Critical thinkers answer the question by flipping the question and making it into a statement or claim.

MATERIALS

- Review & Practice handout (pages 31–32)
- green highlighters (optional)

As students become more familiar with the ACE structure, let them know that they don't have to be tied to specific sentence starters, especially when it comes to the A (answer) component. Instead, they can use words and phrases from a question and flip the question into a statement. This is called the "Flip It" strategy. Most students already know how to do this, but it helps to make the strategy clear and official and to provide them with practice using it. This lesson may be used in all content areas.

Connect

Say to students: *I hope you are starting to see that you can use the ACE structure to answer any type of open-ended question—in any class, in any subject area, maybe even in a debate with your parents. You never know when you might have to justify your answer or provide evidence for your thinking. I want you to be prepared for whatever type of question comes your way, not just the ones I ask in class.*

So far, you've learned to use different sentence starters to **answer** *questions. But you don't have to memorize all those starters. Today, I'm going to teach you a very simple strategy that will help you with the A part of ACE. It's called the "Flip It" strategy, because that is all it is—flipping the question into a statement.*

Teach

Say to students: *You can answer any question by simply taking words and phrases from the question and then "flipping" them back into your response. Then replace the question mark with a period to make it a clear statement. Taking words and phrases from the question is very important because it helps ensure that you are actually answering the question and not going off topic.*

HOW DO I DO THIS?

1. Read and think about the question.
2. Underline key words or phrases in the question.
3. Using those words and phrases, "flip" the question into your answer.
4. Write your "flip it" statement as your A in ACE.
5. Highlight your answer in green (optional).

TEACHER MODEL

Let me give you some examples to show you what I mean.

Q: What is the theme of the story?

Let me read this question carefully: What is the theme of the story? *Hmm, what words or phrases should I use from the question? The important words are "theme of the story." I'm going to underline them to remind me to use those words when I flip the question.*

A: The theme of the story is . . .

See what I did there? Here are a couple more examples.

Q: After analyzing Sara's work on the math problem, was she correct or incorrect?

A: Sara was incorrect about her answer to the math problem.

Q: What inference can be made about the author's purpose?

A: One inference that can be made about the author's purpose is . . .

Partner Practice

Distribute copies of the Review & Practice handout. Then pair up students and say: *With a partner, practice reading each question and answering it using a complete sentence. Be sure to include words and phrases from the question and flip them into a statement. You don't need to know the actual answer. The point of this exercise is for you to practice flipping the question into a statement. You can just use ellipses (. . .) or make up an answer if you don't know it. One partner asks the question, the other practices flipping it, and both of you write down your answer on your handout.*

Allow time for students to work with their partner to complete the activity. As they work, circulate around the room, keeping an eye out for outstanding examples of today's teaching point.

SAMPLE RESPONSES

1) What is your favorite subject in school?

A: My favorite subject in school is . . .

2) After doing the science experiment, what conclusion can you draw?

A: After the science experiment, one conclusion I can draw is . . .

3) How would you describe the character's personality?

A: The character's personality can be described as courageous.

4) If the area of a triangle is 27 square centimeters and its base is 6 cm, what is its height?

A: The height of the triangle is 9 cm.

Now You Try!

Have students practice the Flip It strategy on their own. Students may write their responses either on their Review & Practice handout or in their writer's notebook.

SAMPLE RESPONSES

1) What factors in history led to the American Revolution?

A: Factors that led to the American Revolution included . . .

2) Based on the passage, what inference can you make about the character's family life?

A: An inference I can make about the character's family life is . . .

3) Do you think police should be able to search a person's cell phone without a warrant?

A: <u>I think police should not be able to search a person's cell phone without a warrant.</u>

4) What is one way to solve the problem: 3x + 2 = 11?

A: <u>One way to solve the problem is . . .</u>

5) Why were the Egyptians so obedient to the pharaoh?

A: <u>The Egyptians were so obedient to the pharaoh because . . .</u>

6) Which sentence best illustrates the character's reason for changing his mind?

A: <u>The sentence that best illustrates the character's reason for changing his mind is . . .</u>

7) What is one genetic trait that owners of pugs should be aware of?

A: <u>One genetic trait owners of pugs should be aware of is . . .</u>

Share and Reflect

Invite a few students to share their answers. If necessary, give feedback on grammar points, how to select words from a question and flip them into the answer, and so on. Then have students modify what they have on their papers accordingly.

LESSON 3
ANSWER USING THE "FLIP IT" STRATEGY

Name: _____ Date: _____

TEACHING POINT
Critical thinkers answer the question by flipping the question and making it into a statement or claim.

How Do I Do This?

1. Read and think about the question.
2. Underline key words or phrases in the question.
3. Using those words and phrases, "flip" the question into your answer.
4. Write your "flip it" statement as your A in ACE.
5. Highlight your answer in green (optional).

Teacher Model

Q: What is the <u>theme of the story</u>?

A: The <u>theme of the story</u> is . . .

Q: After analyzing <u>Sara's</u> work on the <u>math problem</u>, was she correct or incorrect?

A: <u>Sara</u> was <u>incorrect</u> about her answer to the <u>math problem</u>.

Q: What <u>inference</u> can be made about the <u>author's purpose</u>?

A: One <u>inference</u> that can be made about the <u>author's purpose</u> is . . .

Partner Practice

With a partner, take turns reading each question and answering it using a complete sentence. Be sure to underline key words and phrases from the question and flip them into a statement. If you don't know the answer, just use ellipses (. . .) or make up an answer.

1) What is your favorite subject in school?

A: _____

2) After doing the science experiment, what conclusion can you draw?

A: _____

3) How would you describe the character's personality?

A: _____

4) If the area of a triangle is 27 square centimeters and its base is 6 cm, what is its height?

A: _____

Now You Try!

Practice the Flip It strategy on your own.

1) What factors in history led to the American Revolution?

A: _____

2) Based on the passage, what inference can you make about the character's family life?

A: _____

3) Do you think police should be able to search a person's cell phone without a warrant?

A: _____

4) What is one way to solve the problem: 3x + 2 = 11?

A: _____

5) Why were the Egyptians so obedient to the pharaoh?

A: _____

6) Which sentence best illustrates the character's reason for changing his mind?

A: _____

7) What is one genetic trait that owners of pugs should be aware of?

A: _____

ACE Short-Response Writing © Grace Long, Scholastic Inc.

LESSON 4
Cite Evidence Using the "Lift the Line" Strategy

TEACHING POINT
Critical thinkers can cite evidence when responding to a text.

MATERIALS

- Review & Practice handout (pages 37–38)
- text of your choice (anything you're currently reading in class)
- yellow highlighter (optional)

This lesson gives students practice in formulating text evidence–based responses. The kind of evidence that can be seen, pointed to, or extracted from a text is what I call "hard evidence." ("Soft evidence"—based on schema, personal experience, observation, and so on—is appropriate for certain genres or assignments, such as discussions, opinion pieces, or debates.) You can use any text, article, or novel your class is currently working on to teach this lesson.

Connect

Say to students: *As we continue to learn how to ACE our responses, I want to share with you specific strategies for how to* **cite evidence** *to make sure you're giving strong support for your answer. Remember, as a lawyer, you want to offer good, relevant evidence for your cases. For example, in a court trial, if you're trying to prove a man is guilty of* *robbery, you're not going to say, "Well, umm . . . my evidence is that I think there are some diamonds in his car. I seem to remember seeing them there the last time I checked." No one would believe you! Now, if you actually had a picture of the stolen diamonds or, better yet, they're in a plastic bag that you could point to, then you would have clear, hard evidence. More people would be convinced.*

You need to do the same thing with your response—you need to "seal it in a bag." You need to show the reader hard evidence. You do this by citing the relevant article, page, or paragraph and then extracting the words and phrases in the text. Let me show you what I mean.

Teach

Say to students: *Today I'm going to teach you how to cite evidence from a text. One way to do this is by using the "Lift the Line" strategy. In Lift the Line, you search the text for a sentence or paragraph that you can use for evidence, "lift the line" from the text, and include the line in your ACE response.*

HOW DO I DO THIS?

1. Reread or skim the text to look for evidence.
   (Highlight the evidence in yellow if you have actual text.
   If text is electronic, most devices allow you to highlight in yellow.)

2. Put your finger on the line.

3. Write down the page or paragraph number.

4. Use exact words and phrases from the text.
   (If you are using a direct quote from a text, make sure to use quotation marks.)

5. Try one of these sentence starters:
   - *On page _____, the text states . . .*
   - *According to the article (or text) . . .*
   - *The author states that . . .*
   - *One example from the text . . .*
   - *In paragraph _____, it states . . .*

TEACHER MODEL

The following question refers to the short story "The Bracelet" by Yoshiko Uchida, but you can create your own question using any text you are currently reading in class. Have students underline the sentence starters as you go over this example. It is also helpful for students to have yellow highlighters to highlight text evidence on the actual text and in this example.

> **Q: What kind of person is Mama from "The Bracelet" (by Yoshiko Uchida)?**
>
> **A:** Mama from "The Bracelet" can be considered an optimistic person.
>
> **C:** On page 71, the text states that Mama was <u>not worried</u> about who would carry their luggage. She states, <u>"Someone will help us . . . don't worry."</u>

Say to students: *Do you notice how I literally lifted lines, words, and phrases from the text to use in the C of my ACE response?*

> **E:** This shows her positive outlook and faith in human society. Despite their unfortunate circumstances, Mama believed someone would come help them carry their luggage.*

Partner Practice

Distribute copies of the Review & Practice handout. Pair up students and say: *Read the passage and the questions. Highlight words and phrases from the text that you can use as evidence for your answer.*

Allow time for students to complete the activity. As they work, circulate around the room, keeping an eye out for outstanding examples of today's teaching point. Afterwards, invite students to share their responses with the class.

SAMPLE RESPONSES

1) Would it be a good idea for humans to raise a baby bird?

A: It would not be a good idea for humans to raise a baby bird.

C: According to the article, <u>a baby bird requires a carefully balanced meal that only bird parents can provide.</u>

E: This is significant because <u>just as human babies can eat and drink only certain foods when they are growing, the same is true for baby birds.</u>

2) Does a baby bird that has fallen from its nest need to be rescued?

A: Surprisingly, a baby bird that has fallen from its nest does not need to be rescued.

C: According to the article, <u>the bird parents will be able to find their baby and get food to it.</u>

E: This is significant because <u>although people may think they are being helpful when they rescue a baby bird, they might make it even harder for the bird's parents to get it the food it needs.</u>

---

* **Note:** This is an example of the elaboration strategy called Explain Why, taught in Lesson 5.

Now You Try!

Use the text you are currently reading in class to pose one or two questions. Depending on how comfortable your students are with using the ACE strategy, you can provide the A and the E and have them practice only the C, or you can have them write the whole ACE response. Remind students to highlight evidence using a yellow highlighter and to practice the Lift the Line strategy. Have students write their responses in their writer's notebook.

Share and Reflect

Invite a few students to share the text evidence they found for their ACE responses. Have students actually point to the part of the text where they "lifted the line" to use as evidence for their responses.

LESSON 4
CITE EVIDENCE USING THE "LIFT THE LINE" STRATEGY

Name: _____ Date: _____

TEACHING POINT
Critical thinkers can cite evidence when responding to a text.

How Do I Do This?

1. Reread or skim the text to look for evidence.
   (Highlight the evidence in yellow if you have actual text. If text is electronic, most devices allow you to highlight in yellow.)

2. Put your finger on the line.

3. Write down the page or paragraph number.

4. Use exact words and phrases from the text.
   (If you are using a direct quote from a text, make sure to use quotation marks.)

5. Try these sentence starters:
   - *On page _____, the text states . . .*
   - *According to the article (or text) . . .*
   - *The author states that . . .*
   - *One example from the text . . .*
   - *In paragraph _____, it states . . .*

Teacher Model

Q: What kind of person is Mama from "The Bracelet" (by Yoshiko Uchida)?

A: Mama from "The Bracelet" can be considered an optimistic person.

C: On page 71, the text states that Mama was <u>not worried</u> about who would carry their luggage. She states, <u>"Someone will help us . . . don't worry."</u>

(Notice how I lifted lines, words, and phrases from the text into my answer.)

E: This shows her positive outlook and faith in human society. Despite their unfortunate circumstances, Mama believed someone would come help them carry their luggage.

Partner Practice

With your partner, read the short passage below. Read the questions, then highlight words and phrases from the text that you can use as evidence for your answers. Practice the "Lift the Line" strategy by writing your responses in ACE format.

Raising Baby Birds

If you spend time outdoors, you may come across a baby bird that has fallen out of its nest. Many people think that they can take a baby bird home and raise it themselves. This is not the case! A baby bird needs to be fed every 15 minutes. Baby birds must eat a carefully balanced meal that usually only bird parents can provide.

The best thing to do if you find a baby bird on the ground is to wait and let the bird's parents find and care for it. The parents are often watching their baby from the bushes, even if you can't see them from where you stand. A baby bird can still survive on the ground if its parents can get food to it.

Reprinted from *Scholastic News.* Copyright © Scholastic Inc.

1) Would it be a good idea for humans to raise a baby bird?

A: It would not be a good idea for humans to raise a baby bird.

C: According to the article, _____

_____

E: This is significant because _____

_____

2) Does a baby bird that has fallen from its nest need to be rescued?

A: Surprisingly, a baby bird that has fallen from its nest does not need to be rescued.

C: According to the article, _____

_____

E: This is significant because _____

_____

PART II
Elaboration Strategies

At this point, students should feel fairly comfortable using the ACE structure to respond to questions. Having learned the "Flip It" and "Lift the Line" strategies in addition to some sentence starters, they usually can generate the A (answer) and C (cite evidence) quite easily.

Many struggle with the E, or elaboration, however. Often, the E sounds like a repeat of the A or C. To help students avoid repetition, the lessons in this section introduce eight elaboration strategies that elicit deeper, critical thinking.

1. Explain Why
2. Cause and Effect
3. Compare and Contrast
4. Real-World Connection
5. Before and After
6. Show Your Voice
7. Say More
8. Visualize It

It is important that students learn the specific name of each strategy and the sentence starters associated with it. Explicitly naming each strategy helps students categorize and organize their thoughts, thereby making their elaboration intentional. Encourage students to use their schema—their personal background knowledge—to make sense of the content presented to them. These lessons guide students on the pathway to critical thinking as they think about the purpose of their evidence, ask themselves questions to activate their thinking, and then access knowledge in their schema to explain and elaborate.

Keep in mind that you don't need to teach the elaboration strategies in the order presented in this book. Some teachers might introduce one E strategy at a time, while others prefer to teach a few together. Depending on the genre or content your class is studying, you'll find that some elaboration strategies might be more applicable than others.

(See the Elaboration Matrix on pages 140–141.) By the time students have learned all eight strategies, they will be able to determine for themselves which strategy to use in each context to suit their needs.

Since these lessons focus on the elaboration strategies and the thinking process behind each one, the activities provide the A and C so students can concentrate on the E. However, feel free to differentiate the activities as needed. For example, you may want to challenge higher-achieving students by having them ACE the entire response on their own, combine elaboration strategies, or maybe even come up with their own strategies. For struggling students, you may want to provide sentence starters or perhaps offer more support through sentence frames. Continue to encourage the use of colored highlighters to help students identify their answer (green), evidence (yellow), and elaboration (pink).

The elaboration strategies are at the heart of the ACE strategy. Get ready to enjoy rich discussion and to be impressed by the critical thinking skills your students will display!

LESSON 5
Using the "Explain Why" Strategy

TEACHING POINT
Critical thinkers can elaborate by using the "Explain Why" strategy.

MATERIALS

- Review & Practice handout (pages 47–49)
- "The Story of the Three Little Pigs" (page 132)
- "Too Plugged In" (page 133)
- pink highlighters
- Elaboration Matrix (pages 140–141)

In this lesson, students learn how to elaborate using the "Explain Why" strategy. Although knowing its name is important, the emphasis should be on its purpose: We use this strategy when we want to *explain why* our evidence is important to our claim. Explain Why is probably the hardest and most abstract of all the strategies. We start with this one because it is also the most universal and can be used to elaborate on almost any genre, topic, or content area.

   Expect students to struggle with elaboration at the beginning. As they learn more elaboration strategies, Explain Why will make more sense. Encourage them to elaborate by using different words and phrases than what is already in the A and C part of their answer.

Connection

Say to students: *We've been practicing using ACE over the last few days, and I think you've got the A and C down. But the part that everyone seems to find a bit more challenging is the E—elaborating on why your evidence is important. With today's rigorous standards, it is no longer good enough to simply give an answer to a question. You have to support your answer with evidence; you have to elaborate; you have to explain your thinking and give reasons for why you think what you think.*

Essentially, that's what lawyers have to do—they prove their point, give evidence, and elaborate on why their thinking is correct. If a lawyer is making a claim that a suspect is guilty (A) and shows a bag filled with stolen diamonds in it (C), is the lawyer done? No. The lawyer still has to elaborate on how and why that evidence makes the suspect guilty. So what? Why is that evidence important? What does it mean that the suspect has stolen diamonds in his car? How does that show he's guilty? You can't assume the reader or the audience can automatically make those connections.

Teach

Say to students: *One way to elaborate upon your evidence is to use the Explain Why strategy. This type of elaboration is exactly what it sounds like—you explain why your evidence is important and how it supports your claim. Let me show you what tends to happen with weak lawyers. We will use the same example as before of the suspect accused of robbery.*

This is what <u>not</u> to do:

A: The suspect is guilty.

C: Stolen diamonds were found in his car.

E: This proves he's guilty.

Notice that the lawyer just repeated what he had already said without offering an explanation. The following is a much more convincing response.

A: The suspect is guilty.

C: Stolen diamonds were found in his car.

E: This is significant because surveillance cameras showed the suspect and his car at the scene of the crime around the time of the robbery.

Do you see how I explained the significance of the evidence? You need to show the reader how the evidence supports your claim. This example relates to a criminal case, but you can use the Explain Why strategy with almost any genre or question.

HOW DO I DO THIS?

1. Read the story or article to understand what it's about.

2. Read the question and think about the topic.

3. Use the Explain Why Boxes to organize your thoughts (see below).

4. Formulate an answer and write it in the A box (may be words, phrases, or sentences).

5. Reread the text to look for evidence that would support your answer. In the C box, record the evidence you find.

6. Elaborate upon your answer using the Explain Why strategy. Ask yourself these questions:
   - *Why is this important?*
   - *Why would this matter to the reader?*
   - *How does this prove that your evidence is related to your claim?*
   - *As a lawyer, how could you convince the jury that your evidence is important?*

7. ACE your response using one of these sentence starters to elaborate.
   - *This shows that . . .*
   - *This is significant because . . .*
   - *As you can see . . .*

EXPLAIN WHY BOXES

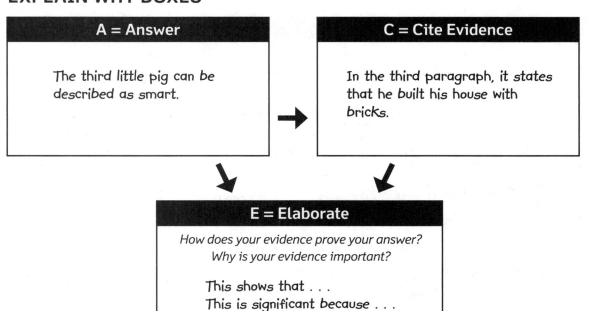

A = Answer	C = Cite Evidence
The third little pig can be described as smart.	In the third paragraph, it states that he built his house with bricks.

E = Elaborate

How does your evidence prove your answer?
Why is your evidence important?

This shows that . . .
This is significant because . . .

TEACHER MODEL

Read aloud "The Story of the Three Little Pigs" (page 132) to the class. (Note: The chosen text for this lesson is intentionally simple. The goal is for students to see a quick, tangible example of the Explain Why strategy being used.) On the board, draw the Explain Why Boxes (page 43) to support the example.

The Story of the Three Little Pigs

Q: How would you describe the third little pig?

A: I would describe the third little pig as smart.

C: In the story, it states that he built his house with bricks.

Say to students: *How does the fact that the third little pig built his house out of bricks show that he is smart? Well, he knew that bricks are much stronger and sturdier than straw or sticks. Neither wind nor the wolf can blow the house down. I'm going to write this in a scholarly way.*

E: This shows that he was thoughtful and wise about what material he used to build his house. He knew that if he built his house with bricks, it would be sturdy and couldn't be blown away.

Partner Practice

Distribute copies of the Review & Practice handout and "The Story of the Three Little Pigs." Then pair up students and say: *Now, practice the Explain Why strategy with your partner. Partner A, read the question and the A and C. Partner B, help prompt your partner's thinking by asking the questions from Step 6 of How Do I Do This? Then try one of the Explain Why sentence starters to write the E.*

Allow time for students to complete the activity. As they work, circulate around the room, keeping an eye out for outstanding examples of today's teaching point. Afterwards, invite students to share their responses with the class.

SAMPLE RESPONSE

Q: How would you describe the third little pig?

A: I would describe the third little pig as smart.

C: In the story, it states that the wolf tried to enter the house through the chimney, but the third little pig put a pot of boiling water under it, so the wolf died.

E: This shows that <u>the third little pig was thinking ahead. He knew the wolf would try to enter the house a different way, so he outsmarted the wolf. This is significant because the three little pigs stayed safe and the wolf died.</u>

Now You Try!

Distribute copies of "Too Plugged In" (page 133). Have students read the article and answer the questions in their Review & Practice handout, using the Explain Why strategy to elaborate. Note that A and C are already given, so students only need to complete E based on the information given and their own reasoning. Remind students not to use the same words or phrases as in A or C. Their goal is to explain how and why the evidence is connected to the answer. Students may write their responses either on the handout or in their writer's notebook.

SAMPLE RESPONSES

(For 1 and 2): Should children have limits on their screen time?

1) A: Yes, children should have limits on their screen time.

   C: According to the article, kids spend about seven hours a day in front of screens.

   E: This is significant because that is a lot of time spent not going outside, getting sun, and doing physical activity.

2) A: No, kids should not have limits on their screen time.

   C: According to the article, watching television and playing video games can be relaxing.

   E: This is significant because in today's day and age, school life can be very stressful and may lead to anxiety. Some relaxation and down time might be just what the brain needs to get ready for the next day.

(For 3 and 4): Are there negative effects from too much screen time?

3) A: There are many negative health impacts from too much screen time.

   C: According to the article, too much screen time can lead to weight gain.

   E: This is significant because weight gain can lead to heart disease, diabetes, and other health problems.

4) A: There are many negative health impacts from too much screen time.

   C: According to the article, kids can have trouble sleeping.

   E: This is significant because sleep is very important for growing children. Sleep allows their bodies and brains to get rest as well as develop.

(For 5 and 6): How can kids utilize technology in a positive way?

5) A: One way to utilize technology in a positive way is to have limited screen time.

    C: In the last paragraph, the article suggests limiting screen time to two hours or less a day.

    E: This is significant because <u>this allows plenty of time for kids to get outside, interact with friends, and get physical exercise.</u>

6) A: One way to reduce the negative impact of technology is to limit screen time right before bed.

    C: According to research, screen time close to bedtime can cause kids to toss and turn as their brains are not completely shut off.

    E: This shows that <u>screen time right before bed is not a good idea because kids are likely to feel tired and cranky the next day.</u>

Share and Reflect

Invite students to share their answers. Remind the class to listen as others share. Then have them write a response to one of these sentence frames:

- *I heard my classmate say _____, and it made me think about _____.*
- *I learned _____.*

LESSON 5
USING THE "EXPLAIN WHY" STRATEGY

Name: _____ Date: _____

How Do I Do This?

1. Read the story or article to understand what it's about.

2. Read the question and think about the topic.

3. Use the Explain Why Boxes to organize your thoughts (see below).

4. Formulate an answer and write it in the A box (may be words, phrases, or sentences).

5. Reread the text to look for evidence that would support your answer.
In the C box, record the evidence you find.

6. Elaborate upon your answer using the Explain Why strategy. Ask yourself these questions:
- Why is this important?
- Why would this matter to the reader?
- How does this prove that your evidence is related to your claim?
- As a lawyer, how could you convince the jury that your evidence is important?

7. ACE your response using one of these sentence starters to elaborate.
- *This shows that . . .*
- *This is significant because . . .*
- *As you can see . . .*

Explain Why Boxes

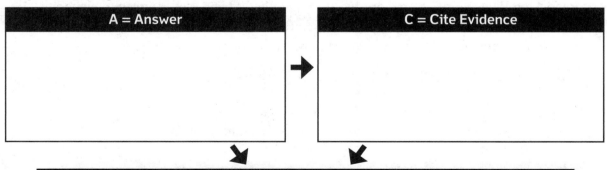

A = Answer	C = Cite Evidence

E = Elaborate

How does your evidence prove your answer? Why is your evidence important?

This shows that . . .

This is significant because . . .

Teacher Model

The Story of the Three Little Pigs

Q: How would you describe the third little pig?

A: I would describe the third little pig as smart.

C: In the story, it states that he built his house with bricks.

E: This shows that he was thoughtful and wise about what material he used to build his house. He knew that if he built his house with bricks, it would be sturdy and couldn't be blown away.

Partner Practice

Read "The Story of the Three Little Pigs" (from your teacher). Then work with a partner to practice the Explain Why strategy. Read the question and the given A and C. Then use one of the sentence starters from Step 7 of How Do I Do This? to elaborate.

Q: How would you describe the third little pig?

A: I would describe the third little pig as smart.

C: In the story, it states that the wolf tried to enter the house through the chimney, but the third little pig put a pot of boiling water under it, so the wolf died.

Think and discuss: *How does this evidence prove that the third little pig is smart? What does this piece of evidence tell you about the pig?*

E: This shows that _____

_____

Now You Try!

Read "Too Plugged In" (from your teacher). Use the Explain Why strategy to elaborate. Note that A and C are already given, so fill in E based on that information and your own reasoning. Remember: Do not use the same words or phrases in A or C.

(For 1 and 2): Should children have limits on their screen time?

1) **A:** Yes, children should have limits on their screen time.

   C: According to the article, kids spend about seven hours a day in front of screens.

   E: This is significant because _____

_____

2) A: No, kids should not have limits on their screen time.

C: According to the article, watching television and playing video games can be relaxing.

E: This is significant because _____

_____

(For 3 and 4): Are there negative effects from too much screen time?

3) A: There are many negative health impacts from too much screen time.

C: According to the article, too much screen time can lead to weight gain.

E: This is significant because _____

_____

4) A: There are many negative health impacts from too much screen time.

C: According to the article, kids can have trouble sleeping.

E: This is significant because _____

_____

(For 5 and 6): How can kids utilize technology in a positive way?

5) A: One way to utilize technology in a positive way is to have limited screen time.

C: In the last paragraph, the article suggests limiting screen time to two hours or less a day.

E: This is significant because _____

_____

6) A: One way to reduce the negative impact of technology time is to limit screen time right before bed.

C: According to research, screen time close to bedtime can cause kids to toss and turn as their brains are not completely shut off.

E: This shows that _____

_____

LESSON 6
Using the "Cause and Effect" Strategy

TEACHING POINT
Critical thinkers can elaborate by using the "Cause and Effect" strategy.

MATERIALS

- Review & Practice handout (pages 56–58)
- "The Story of the Three Little Pigs" (page 132)
- "Too Plugged In" (page 133)
- pink highlighters (optional)

The "Cause and Effect" elaboration strategy is more concrete than Explain Why, so students tend to enjoy using it. Cause and Effect is especially useful for argumentative writing, essay writing, response to nonfiction text, math, science, and social studies. The examples used in this lesson are intentionally simple and general to accommodate multiple grade levels. You can also teach this strategy using a text or novel you are reading in your class.

Connect

Say to students: *Thinkers, you've done a great job using the Explain Why strategy to elaborate your responses. Like critical thinkers, you are learning how to use your own knowledge to prove your point. We will be studying a total of eight elaboration strategies so as we learn new ones make sure you don't forget about the ones you've already learned.*

I've noticed that your As and Cs come easily to you, but when it comes to your E, there seems to be a struggle. Oftentimes, it seems like your E is just a repeat of your A and C.

Today we are going to learn another elaboration strategy. How many of you have played with dominoes before? Imagine that you line up as many dominoes as you can. What will happen if you tip the first one? (They will all get knocked down.) *What was the cause?* (A finger pushed the first domino.) *What was the effect?* (All the dominoes fell down.) *We are going to use this concept of "cause and effect" as an elaboration strategy.*

Note: For younger grades, the picture book *If You Give a Mouse a Cookie* by Laura Numeroff is a great way to introduce cause and effect.

Teach

Say to students: *The elaboration strategy we will study today is called "Cause and Effect." Some of you may have used this strategy already but didn't know it. "Cause and effect" means that if something happens (cause), other things happen because of it (effects). In terms of ACE, if we make a claim (A), and we believe our evidence (C) is important, we can elaborate (E) by thinking about the causes and effects of that evidence. We can use a Cause and Effect flowchart to help organize our thinking* (see below).

Let's talk through an example. Let's say a student never does her homework. (Write this in the Cause box.) *What are some of the possible effects of not doing homework?* (Call on student volunteers.) *What are the consequences of that?* (Record students' responses in the Effect boxes.)

CAUSE AND EFFECT FLOWCHART

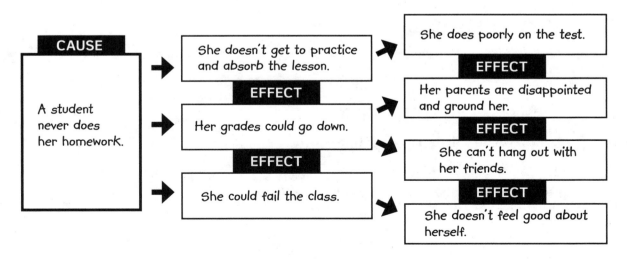

As you can see, the Cause and Effect flowchart helps us organize our thoughts so we can construct an ACE response. Here's what it might look like:

Q: Should homework be counted as part of your grade?

A: Homework should not be counted as part of the grade.

C: One reason is that it could impact a student's self-esteem in a negative way.

E: If a student constantly misses homework, **then** her grades will go down. **If** this happens, **then** she might get discouraged and simply stop trying.

Now that we've reviewed the concept of cause and effect, let's discuss how you would use this concept to elaborate.

HOW DO I DO THIS?

1. Use a Cause and Effect flowchart to organize your thoughts.

2. Write the A in your Cause box.

3. Push your thinking and ask yourself:
   - *What are the effects of this issue?*
   - *What are the consequences of _____?*
   - *If this happens, then what?*

4. Jot down effects in the Effect boxes.

5. ACE your response using one of these sentence starters to elaborate.
   - *One effect of _____ is . . .*
   - *If _____, then . . .*
   - *Due to _____, . . .*
   - *One impact _____ might/would . . .*

TEACHER MODEL

Let's take a look at the example we have used before with "The Story of the Three Little Pigs."

The Story of the Three Little Pigs

Q: How would you describe the third little pig?

A: I would describe the third little pig as smart.

C: In the story, it states that he built his house with bricks.

Think aloud: *How does this show he is smart? What would have happened if he didn't make this choice?*

E: **If** he hadn't built his house out of bricks, **then** the wolf would have been able to blow the house down and gobble up all three pigs.

Say to students: *Do you see that I used the sentence starter "If . . . then . . ." to prompt my thinking about cause and effect? Let's take a look at another example, this time using the "Too Plugged In" article from the previous lesson.*

Too Plugged In

Q: Should children have limits on their screen time?

A: Children should have limits on their screen time.

C: According to the article, American kids spend an average of seven hours a day looking at their screens.

Think aloud: *What happens if you spend that much time looking at your screen? What is an effect on your body, for example?*

E: **One effect of** kids spending that much time looking at their screens is that the kids don't get enough physical exercise.

Say to students: *Do you see how I used the sentence starter "One effect of . . ." to prompt my thinking?*

Partner Practice

Distribute copies of the Review & Practice handout. Then pair up students and say: *Practice the Cause and Effect elaboration strategy with a partner. Partner A asks the question, and Partner B reads the A and C. Then Partner A asks questions from Step 3 of How Do I Do This? to prompt thinking. Both students choose a sentence starter and elaborate.*

Allow time for students to complete the activity. As they work, circulate around the room, keeping an eye out for outstanding examples of today's teaching point. Afterwards, invite students to share their responses with the class.

SAMPLE RESPONSE

Q: Should homework be counted toward a student's grade?

A: Yes, I think homework should be counted toward a student's grade.

C: One reason is that it will motivate students to do their homework consistently.

E: One effect of <u>doing homework consistently is that students get to practice the concepts and skills they learned in class so they understand the lesson better.</u>

Now You Try!

Have students answer the questions on their Review & Practice handout, using the Cause and Effect strategy to elaborate. Students may write their responses either on the handout or in their writer's notebook.

SAMPLE RESPONSES

1) Should homework be counted toward a student's grade?

A: No, homework should not be counted toward a student's grade.

C: One reason is that every student's home environment is different.

E: One impact this may have <u>is that students might get lower grades because they don't have help at home. This would be an unfair consequence.</u>

2) Should soda be allowed at school?

A: No, soda should not be allowed at school.

C: According to research, one can of soda may contain more than five teaspoons of sugar.

E: One effect of <u>too much sugar is that it can cause obesity and diabetes.</u>

3) Should soda be allowed at school?

A: Yes, soda should be allowed at school.

C: According to research, small amounts of caffeine found in soda can increase energy and concentration.

E: If <u>a student can concentrate in class,</u> **then** <u>he or she is more likely to behave well and get better grades.</u>

4) Should students be allowed to bring cell phones to class?

A: Yes, students should be allowed to have cell phones in class.

C: One reason is that they can use their phones to do research.

E: One effect of <u>having information readily available on cell phones is that it can save time from having to pass out computers or books to everyone.</u>

5) Should students be allowed to bring cell phones to class?

A: No, students should not be allowed to bring cell phones to class.

C: One reason is that having phones in class can be a major distraction from student learning.

E: If <u>students are constantly looking down at their phones or texting in class,</u> **then** <u>they are not focusing on the lesson.</u>

6) Should students recycle in school?

A: Yes, students should recycle at school.

C: According to research, we are running out of landfill space.

E: One effect of <u>recycling is that less waste goes to landfills.</u>

Share and Reflect

Invite students to share their answers. Remind the class to pay attention as others share. Then have them write a response using this frame:

- *A sentence starter I heard my friend use was _____.*

LESSON 6

USING THE "CAUSE AND EFFECT" STRATEGY

Name: _____ Date: _____

> **TEACHING POINT**
> Critical thinkers can elaborate by using the "Cause and Effect" strategy.

How Do I Do This?

1. Use a Cause and Effect flowchart (below) to organize your thoughts.

2. Write the A in your Cause box.

3. Push your thinking and ask yourself:

- What are the effects of this issue?
- What are the consequences of _____?
- If this happens, then what?

4. Jot down effects in the Effect boxes.

5. ACE your response using one of these sentence starters to elaborate.

- *One effect of _____ is . . .*
- *If _____, then . . .*
- *Due to _____, . . .*
- *One impact _____ might/would . . .*

Cause and Effect Flowchart

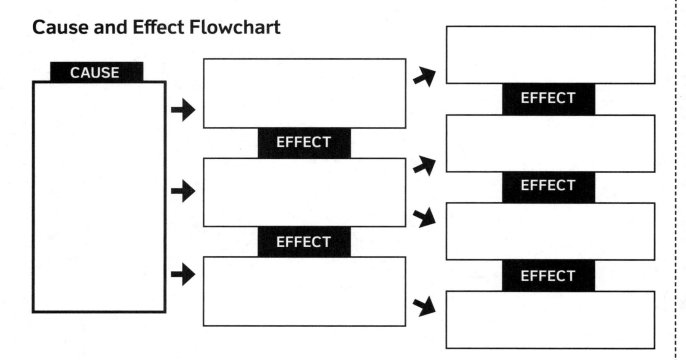

Teacher Model

The Story of the Three Little Pigs

Q: How would you describe the third little pig?

A: I would describe the third little pig as smart.

C: In the story, it states that he built his house with bricks.

E: If he hadn't built his house out of bricks, **then** the wolf would have been able to blow the house down and gobble up all three pigs.

Too Plugged In

Q: Should children have limits on their screen time?

A: Children should have limits on their screen time.

C: According to the article, American kids spend an average of seven hours a day looking at their screens.

E: One effect of kids spending that much time looking at their screens is that the kids don't get enough physical exercise.

Partner Practice

Work with a partner to practice the Cause and Effect elaboration strategy. Partner A asks the question, and Partner B reads the A and C. Then Partner A asks questions from Step 3 of the How Do I Do This? to prompt thinking. Choose a sentence starter from Step 5 to elaborate.

Q: Should homework be counted toward a student's grade?

A: Yes, I think homework should be counted toward a student's grade.

C: One reason is that it will motivate students to do their homework consistently.

E: One effect of _____

_____

Now You Try!

Use the Cause and Effect strategy to elaborate. Note that the A and C are already given, so use that information along with your own reasoning to fill in E.

1) Should homework be counted toward a student's grade?

A: No, homework should not be counted toward a student's grade.

C: One reason is that every student's home environment is different.

E: One impact this may have _____

_____

2) Should soda be allowed at school?

A: No, soda should not be allowed at school.

C: According to research, one can of soda may contain more than five teaspoons of sugar.

E: One effect of _____

_____

3) Should soda be allowed at school?

A: Yes, soda should be allowed at school.

C: According to research, small amounts of caffeine found in soda can increase energy and concentration.

E: If _____ ,

then _____

4) Should students be allowed to bring cell phones to class?

A: Yes, students should be allowed to have cell phones in class.

C: One reason is that they can use their phones to do research.

E: One effect of _____

_____

5) Should students be allowed to bring cell phones to class?

A: No, students should not be allowed to bring cell phones to class.

A: One reason is that having phones in class can be a major distraction from student learning.

E: If _____ ,

then _____

6) Should students recycle in school?

A: Yes, students should recycle at school.

C: According to research, we are running out of landfill space.

E: One effect of _____

_____

LESSON 7
Using the "Compare and Contrast" Strategy

TEACHING POINT

Critical thinkers can elaborate by using the "Compare and Contrast" strategy.

MATERIALS

- Review & Practice handout (pages 64–66)
- "The Story of the Three Little Pigs" (page 132)
- "The Dove and the Ant" (page 133)
- pink highlighters (optional)

The "Compare and Contrast" elaboration strategy is especially useful for literary response, character analysis, content areas, and argumentative writing.

Remind students to always say the name of the strategy they are using. This will help them to remember the thinking that goes with it.

Connect

Say to students: *You're getting really good at ACE'ing your responses. I can see you really push your thinking when you use the elaboration strategies we've studied so far. Remember, elaboration is the critical component of ACE because you are making it clear why the evidence supports your claim. The kind of thinking we are going to do today is similar to the type of thinking you may have done in the past with Venn diagrams or double-bubble maps.*

Teach

Say to students: *Today we are going to learn another way to elaborate, using the Compare and Contrast strategy. How many of you have heard of "compare and contrast"? What exactly are we doing when we compare and contrast? We're thinking about similarities and differences between two or more things. When we think about differences, it's kind of like thinking of opposites. Thinking of the opposite or what could have been or what a character did or did not do is often a great way to elaborate upon your evidence.*

For example, if I want to make a claim that Mrs. Smith is the best teacher in the school, I could ACE it and say:

A: Mrs. Smith is the best teacher in the school.

C: One reason is that she explains every lesson in multiple ways.

E: Unlike some teachers who teach a lesson once and move on, Mrs. Smith reteaches the lesson a different way if students don't get it the first time.

Notice that I thought of the opposite of what Mrs. Smith does. It helped me to use the sentence starter "Unlike _____, . . ."

HOW DO I DO THIS?

1. Write down your A and C (your claim and evidence).

2. Push your thinking and ask yourself:
- *How is _____ the same as or different from other _____?*
- *What does _____ do that's different from what others do?*
- *What's the opposite of _____?*
- *What makes _____ unique or different from others?*

3. ACE your response using one of these sentence starters to elaborate.
- *Most _____, but . . .*
- *Unlike _____, . . .*
- *_____ could have _____, but instead . . .*

TEACHER MODEL

Let's look again at the example we've used before—"The Story of the Three Little Pigs." (Note: The text is intentionally simple, so students can quickly see a tangible example of the Compare and Contrast strategy. Alternatively, you can use any text from your classroom as an example.)

The Story of the Three Little Pigs

Students may find it helpful to have the actual text (page 132) in front of them so they can practice pointing to the text as they find evidence.

Q: How would you describe the third little pig?

A: I would describe the third little pig as smart.

C: In the story, it states that he built his house with bricks.

E: Unlike the other two little pigs, the third little pig put some thought into what material would last.

Say to students: *Did you notice that I used the Compare and Contrast strategy by thinking about how the third little pig was different from the two other pigs? I also could have said, "The third little pig could have done the same thing as the two other pigs and just picked the simplest materials, but instead he chose the sturdiest one that would make a good, strong house."*

Partner Practice

Distribute copies of the Review & Practice handout and "The Story of the Three Little Pigs." Then pair up students and say: *With your partner, look at each question and read the given A and C. Then try one of the Compare and Contrast sentence starters to write the E. If you or your partner is stuck, prompt each other by asking questions from Step 2 of How Do I Do This?*

Allow time for students to complete the activity. As they work, circulate around the room, keeping an eye out for outstanding examples of today's teaching point. Afterwards, invite students to share their responses with the class.

SAMPLE RESPONSES

1) How would you describe the first little pig?

A: I would describe the first little pig as lazy.

C: According to the story, he built his house quickly out of straw and then sang and danced the rest of the day.

E: <u>Unlike the third little pig, who worked hard all day, the first little pig just took the easiest way to make a house so he could go back to playing.</u>

2) How would you describe the wolf?

A: I would describe the wolf as persistent.

C: According to the story, the wolf kept trying to blow down the third house for a long time.

E: <u>The wolf could have given up after a few tries, but instead he just kept blowing until he was out of breath.</u>

Now You Try!

Distribute copies of "The Dove and the Ant" (page 133). Have students read the story and answer the questions on their Review & Practice handout, using the Compare and Contrast strategy to elaborate. Students may write their responses either on the handout or in their writer's notebook.

SAMPLE RESPONSES

1) In the story "The Dove and the Ant," how would you describe the dove?

A: I would describe the dove as compassionate.

C: In the story, when the dove saw that the ant was getting washed away by the river, she dropped a small branch into the water so the ant could use it to get back to shore.

E: <u>The dove could have just ignored the ant since they hardly knew each other, but instead she went out of her way to save him.</u>

2) In the story "The Dove and the Ant," how would you describe the ant?

A: I would describe the ant as grateful.

C: In the story, when the ant saw that a hunter was aiming his bow toward the dove who had rescued him, he stung the hunter on the foot.

E: <u>The ant could have walked away, but instead he remembered that the dove had saved him earlier and attacked the hunter to save the dove in return.</u>

3) Which superhero do you think is the best?

A: I think Batman is the best superhero.

C: One reason is that Batman doesn't have actual superpowers.

E: <u>Unlike other superheroes, Batman relies on his own human strength and intelligence to fight and outwit villains.</u>

4) Which do you think is better—e-books or print books?

A: I think e-books are better than print books.

C: One reason is that one small device can hold many books.

E: Unlike print books, which can take up a lot of space inside your bag, e-books take up only memory space in one device.

5) Who is someone you admire?

A: My mom is a person I admire.

C: One reason is that she works full time and goes to school at night to get her college degree.

E: My mom could have decided she didn't need to finish college because she already has a job, but instead she decided to go back to school so she can have better job opportunities when she graduates.

Share and Reflect

Invite students to share their answers. Remind the class to listen carefully and pay attention as others share. Then have them write a response using this frame:

- *When _____ (classmate) used the Compare and Contrast strategy, it made me think about _____.*

LESSON 7

USING THE "COMPARE AND CONTRAST" STRATEGY

Name: _____ Date: _____

TEACHING POINT

Critical thinkers can elaborate by using the "Compare and Contrast" strategy.

How Do I Do This?

1. Write down your A and C (your claim and evidence).

2. Push your thinking and ask yourself:

- How is _____ the same as or different from other _____?
- What does _____ do that's different from what others do?
- What's the opposite of _____?
- What makes _____ unique or different from others?

3. ACE your response using one of these sentence starters to elaborate.

- *Most _____, but . . .*
- *Unlike _____, . . .*
- *_____ could have _____, but instead . . .*

Teacher Model

The Story of the Three Little Pigs

Q: How would you describe the third little pig?

A: I would describe the third little pig as smart.

C: In the story, it states that he built his house with bricks.

E: Unlike the other two little pigs, the third little pig put some thought into what material would last.

Partner Practice

Read "The Story of the Three Little Pigs" (from your teacher). Then work with a partner to practice the Compare and Contrast strategy. Read each question and the given A and C. Then use one of the sentence starters from Step 3 of How Do I Do This? to elaborate.

1) How would you describe the first little pig?

A: I would describe the first little pig as lazy.

C: According to the story, he built his house quickly out of straw and then sang and danced the rest of the day.

E: _____

_____

2) How would you describe the wolf?

A: I would describe the wolf as persistent.

C: According to the story, the wolf kept trying to blow down the third house for a long time.

E: _____

_____

Now You Try!

Read "The Dove and the Ant" (from your teacher) and the questions below. Use the Compare and Contrast strategy to elaborate. Note that the A and C are already given, so use that information along with your own reasoning to fill in E.

1) In the story "The Dove and the Ant," how would you describe the dove?

A: I would describe the dove as compassionate.

C: In the story, when the dove saw that the ant was getting washed away by the river, she dropped a small branch into the water so the ant could use it to get back to shore.

E: _____

_____

2) In the story "The Dove and the Ant," how would you describe the ant?

A: I would describe the ant as grateful.

C: In the story, when the ant saw that a hunter was aiming his bow toward the dove who had rescued him, he stung the hunter on the foot.

E: _____

_____

3) Which superhero do you think is the best?

A: I think Batman is the best superhero.

C: One reason is that Batman doesn't have actual superpowers.

E: _____

_____

4) Which do you think is better—e-books or print books?

A: I think e-books are better than print books.

C: One reason is that one small device can hold many books.

E: _____

_____

5) Who is someone you admire?

A: My mom is a person I admire.

C: One reason is that she works full time and goes to school at night to get her college degree.

E: _____

_____

LESSON 8
Using the "Real-World Connection" Strategy

MATERIALS

- Review & Practice handout (pages 72–74)
- "The Story of the Three Little Pigs" (page 132)
- "Two Hands on the Paddle" (page 134)
- pink highlighters (optional)

As its name implies, the "Real-World Connection" elaboration strategy is about making connections (an important reading comprehension skill) and using analogies to show how the evidence supports the claim. It is especially applicable for content areas such as science, math, and history. This strategy is also great for literary analysis and argumentative writing.

Connect

Say to students: *You're becoming experts at ACE'ing your responses. As a reminder,* elaboration *means going deeper into your thinking and explaining why the evidence is important to your claim. I encourage you to continue using the elaboration strategies you've learned so far to explain your thinking when making a claim.*

Teach

Say to students: *Today I'm going to challenge you to learn another strategy called "Real-World Connection." I think you're going to like this strategy because it encourages you to call on all your knowledge and schema from school and outside of school. Can anyone tell me what it means to make a connection to something?* (Call on some student volunteers to share their thinking). *When you make a connection to a text, a character, a subject, or anything else, you are thinking about something that reminds you of your current topic.*

You are all smart, knowledgeable students who learn a lot from the world around you—from your family, parents, TV, the news, other teachers, your extracurricular activities. This is all knowledge in your schema. When you use the Real-World Connection strategy, you are using all the knowledge you already have to connect to the topic.

Let me show you what I mean. For example, if I want to make a claim that Mrs. Smith is the best teacher in the school, I could ACE it and say:

A: Mrs. Smith is the best teacher in the school.

C: One reason is that she explains things in multiple ways.

E: This reminds me of what our math teacher tells us to do—try different ways to solve a problem until you find a way that works for you.

Say to students: *Did you notice that I used my existing knowledge of a previous math class and connected it to my evidence? Here's another example:*

A: People should never text and drive at the same time.

C: According to DMV.org, texting while driving is one of the leading causes of death in teens.

Think aloud: *What in my schema do I already know about distracted driving? Where have I seen a similar scenario where a person's chances of getting into an accident are higher because of a poor choice? I know! Drunk driving is dangerous, and I know it causes more accidents. I'm going to use this connection for my elaboration.*

E: This is similar to drunk driving, which accounted for more than a quarter of all traffic-related deaths in 2016.

HOW DO I DO THIS?

1. Write down your A and C (your claim and evidence).

2. Push your thinking and ask yourself:

- *Does this _____ remind you of another _____?*
- *Has there been an issue or topic that you've heard of somewhere (for example, in the news) that can help explain your claim?*
- *Can you think of an analogy to explain your point? (for upper grades)*

3. ACE your response using one of these sentence starters to elaborate.

- *This is similar to . . .*
- *This reminds me of . . .*
- *In the real world, this is like . . .*
- *A similar scenario would be . . .*

TEACHER MODEL

Let's take a look at the example we have used before with "The Story of the Three Little Pigs." (Note: It may seem redundant to keep using the same story, but using similar texts highlights how we can use different strategies to elaborate our responses.)

The Story of the Three Little Pigs

Q: How would you describe the third little pig?

A: I would describe the third little pig as smart.

C: In the story, it states that he worked hard all day to build his house with bricks.

Think aloud: *Can I think of another scenario in which someone was smart because he took his time to build something solid rather than do a quicker job? This makes me think of the Egyptians who built the Great Pyramid thousands of years ago. Historians say it took them about 20 years to build the pyramid, and it still stands today! I'm going to use this connection.*

E: This reminds me of the ancient Egyptians, who took 20 years to build the Great Pyramid. It still stands today, even after thousands of years.

Did you notice that I used the Real-World Connection strategy to show how my evidence supports my claim? Other elaboration sentences I could have used might include:

- **In the real world,** people who work hard and smart are often successful.
- **This reminds me of** the time I got an A+ on my test. I was the last one to finish, but that was because I checked and rechecked all my answers. It paid off!

Partner Practice

Distribute copies of the Review & Practice handout and "The Story of the Three Little Pigs" (page 132). Then pair up students and say: *With a partner, look at the questions. Read the A and C and then try one of the Real-World Connection sentence starters. If you or your partner is stuck, ask questions from Step 2 of How Do I Do This? to help prompt thinking.*

Allow time for students to complete the activity. As they work, circulate around the room, keeping an eye out for outstanding examples of today's teaching point. Afterwards, invite students to share their responses with the class.

SAMPLE RESPONSES

1) How would you describe the first little pig?

A: I would describe the first little pig as lazy.

C: According to the story, he built his house quickly out of straw and then sang and danced the rest of the day.

E: This reminds me of the saying, "Haste makes waste."

2) How would you describe the wolf?

A: I would describe the wolf as persistent.

C: According to the story, the wolf kept trying to blow down the third house for a long time.

E: This is similar to my little brother, who keeps trying to shoot the basketball into the hoop over our garage door, even though he never gets the ball in.

Now You Try!

Distribute copies of "Two Hands on the Paddle" (page 134). Have students read the story and answer the questions in their Review & Practice handout, using Real-World Connection to elaborate. Tell students: *Some of the questions and answers are the same as in the previous activity, so you can see that we can use different elaboration strategies to answer the same questions.*

SAMPLE RESPONSES

1) In the story "Two Hands on the Paddle," how would you describe Uncle Sid?

A: I would describe Uncle Sid as responsible.

C: In the story, Uncle Sid talked to the kids about safety before they went kayaking.

E: This reminds me of when we have fire and safety drills in school, so we know what to do in case of a real emergency.

2) In the story "Two Hands on the Paddle," why do you think Uncle Sid took Brenda and Brandon kayaking?

A: I think Uncle Sid took Brenda and Brandon kayaking so he could spend time with them and they could bond together.

C: In the story, Uncle Sid and the kids paddled together and he took them to his favorite spot, Ice Fort Cove.

E: A similar scenario would be when parents take their kids on an outing, such as to the zoo or a park, so they can hang out together and do things together as a family.

3) Which superhero do you think is the best?

A: I think Batman is the best superhero.

C: One reason is that Batman doesn't have actual superpowers.

E: This would be like a firefighter who uses his natural strength to rescue people from a burning building.

4) Which do you think is better—e-books or print books?

A: I think e-books are better than print books.

C: One reason is that one small device can hold many books.

E: This is similar to having a smartphone, which includes many other apps so people can go online, watch videos, play games, listen to music, and many other things.

5) Who is someone you admire?

A: My mom is a person I admire.

C: One reason is that she works full time and goes to school at night to get her college degree.

E: This reminds me of some professional athletes who continue to train and push themselves even in the off-season because they want to make themselves better.

Share and Reflect

Invite students to share their answers. Ask students to listen for their favorite real-world connection. Then have them write a response using the following frame.

- *The most interesting connection I heard came from _____.*
- *He or she shared about _____.*

LESSON 8

USING THE "REAL-WORLD CONNECTION" STRATEGY

Name: _____ Date: _____

TEACHING POINT
Critical thinkers can elaborate by using the "Real-World Connection" strategy.

How Do I Do This?

1. Write down your A and C (your claim and evidence).

2. Push your thinking and ask yourself:

- Does this _____ remind you of another _____?
- Has there been an issue or topic that you've heard of somewhere (for example, in the news) that can help explain your claim?
- Can you think of an analogy to explain your point? (for upper grades)

3. ACE your response using one of these sentence starters to elaborate.

- *This is similar to . . .*
- *This reminds me of . . .*
- *In the real world, this is like . . .*
- *A similar scenario would be . . .*

Teacher Model
The Story of the Three Little Pigs

Q: How would you describe the third little pig?

A: I would describe the third little pig as smart.

C: In the story, it states that he worked hard all day to build his house with bricks.

E: This reminds me of the ancient Egyptians, who took 20 years to build the Great Pyramid. It still stands today, even after thousands of years.

Partner Practice

Read "The Story of the Three Little Pigs" (from your teacher). Work with your partner to practice the Real-World Connection strategy. Read each question and the given A and C. Then use one of the sentence starters from Step 3 of How Do I Do This? to elaborate. If you or partner is stuck, prompt each other by asking questions from Step 2.

1) How would you describe the first little pig?

A: I would describe the first little pig as lazy.

C: According to the story, he built his house quickly out of straw and then sang and danced the rest of the day.

E: _____

_____

2) How would you describe the wolf?

A: I would describe the wolf as persistent.

C: According to the story, the wolf kept trying to blow down the third house for a long time.

E: _____

_____

Now You Try!

Read "Two Hands on the Paddle" (from your teacher) and the questions below. Use the Real-World Connection strategy to elaborate. Note that the A and C are already given, so use that information along with your own reasoning to fill in E.

1) In the story "Two Hands on the Paddle," how would you describe Uncle Sid?

A: I would describe Uncle Sid as responsible.

C: In the story, Uncle Sid talked to the kids about safety before they went kayaking.

E: _____

_____

2) In the story "Two Hands on the Paddle," why do you think Uncle Sid took Brenda and Brandon kayaking?

A: I think Uncle Sid took Brenda and Brandon kayaking so he could spend time with them and they could bond together.

C: In the story, Uncle Sid and the kids paddled together and he took them to his favorite spot, Ice Fort Cove.

E: _____

_____

3) Which superhero do you think is the best?

A: I think Batman is the best superhero.

C: One reason is that Batman doesn't have actual superpowers.

E: _____

_____

4) Which do you think is better—e-books or print books?

A: I think e-books are better than print books.

C: One reason is that one small device can hold many books.

E: _____

_____

5) Who is someone you admire?

A: My mom is a person I admire.

C: One reason is that she works full time and goes to school at night to get her college degree.

E: _____

_____

LESSON 9
Using the "Before and After" Strategy

TEACHING POINT

Critical thinkers can elaborate by using the "Before and After" strategy.

MATERIALS

- Review & Practice handout (pages 81–83)
- "Bigger and Better" (page 134)
- "Before Smartphones" (page 135)
- pink highlighters (optional)

Students learn to elaborate by thinking about time and how things change over time. The "Before and After" strategy is especially helpful for thinking about character development in narratives, events in history, or science experiments. It might help students if they think of this strategy as a more specific variation of the Compare and Contrast strategy.

Connect

Say to students: *Scholars, you've been doing a lot of critical thinking. That means you've been more thoughtful about your thinking and making choices about how you're going to show your knowledge. I want you to start thinking about when it would be appropriate to use each of the elaboration strategies you've learned so far. I also challenge you to combine different elaboration strategies as you see fit. Remember, you are like lawyers. The clearer you can make your argument and elaborate your thinking, the more your audience will comprehend your point of view and believe your claims are credible.*

To get us thinking about the Before and After strategy, let's consider this scenario. How many of you have a younger brother or sister? Do you remember what life was like before your sibling was born? (Invite students to share their experiences.) *You probably had your own room, or perhaps your parents spent more time with you, or maybe you didn't have someone messing with your toys, and so on. Then your little brother or sister came along. What happened then? How did life change?* (Encourage student volunteers to describe.) *When you think of life before and after your little brother or sister was born, you are using the Before and After strategy.*

Teach

Say to students: *The Before and After strategy is similar to Compare and Contrast, but it focuses specifically on differences between time periods, such as historical versus modern times, or changes that have occurred in a given scenario, such as at the beginning and end of a situation, event, or book.*

Here is an example of using the Before and After strategy for a claim about why cell phones should not be allowed in the classroom.

A: Cell phones should not be allowed in the classroom.

C: They are a distraction in many classroom learning environments.

E: Before cell phones existed, schools ran smoothly with just landlines, **but now** cell phones have become a problem as students are using them all the time for social reasons.

As you can see, Before and After is another effective way to elaborate your thinking when you are trying to prove a point or make a claim. Here's another example:

A: Mrs. Smith is the best teacher in the school.

C: Because of her, my grades are now higher than they ever were.

E: Before, I used to get Cs in math class, **but now** that she has explained the concepts more clearly, I get As in math.

Did you notice how I thought about the situation before and how it has changed? That is what the Before and After strategy is about—thinking about the change that has occurred.

HOW DO I DO THIS?

1. Write down your A and C (your claim and evidence).

2. Push your thinking and ask yourself:
   - *What was the character like at the beginning of the book? What was the character like after _____ (event) in the book? What was the character like at the end of the book?*
   - *What was life like before and after _____ (event)?*
   - *What has changed since _____ (event) happened?*
   - *How was life in _____ (period of history) compared to how life is now?*

3. ACE your response by using one of these sentence starters to elaborate.
   - *Before . . . but after (or now) . . .*
   - *In historical times . . . but in modern times . . .*
   - *Historically . . . but in today's society . . .*
   - *At the beginning . . . but by the end . . .*

TEACHER MODEL

Let's take a look at an example using an article about how televisions have changed. Distribute copies of "Bigger and Better" (page 134).

Bigger and Better

Q: How has television changed from when it first appeared?

A: Television has changed by becoming more accessible.

C: According to the article, every decade has brought vast improvements in television and people's ability to enjoy shows.

E: Before, "a fortunate few" viewed a show on a 2-by-3-inch, black-and-white screen, **but now,** with hundreds of channels available and high-definition TVs linked to the internet, people can watch anything they like anytime and anywhere.

Do you notice how I used the Before and After strategy to show how my evidence supports my claim? Keep in mind that elaboration can be more than one sentence. It's also a good idea to combine multiple elaboration strategies to prove your point.

Partner Practice

Distribute copies of the Review & Practice handout. Then pair up students and say: *With your partner, look at each question and read the given A and C. Then try one of the Before and After sentence starters to write the E. If you or your partner is stuck, prompt each other by asking questions from Step 2 in How Do I Do This?*

Allow time for students to complete the activity. As they work, circulate around the room, keeping an eye out for outstanding examples of today's teaching point. Afterwards, invite students to share their responses with the class.

SAMPLE RESPONSES

1) Has technology improved our way of life?

A: Technology has improved our way of life.

C: One reason is that now we have access to so much information in the palm of our hand.

E: <u>Before, people had to go to the library and take out many books to do research. Now, we can access many different kinds of resources on our phones.</u>

2) Has technology improved our way of life?

A: Technology has not improved our way of life.

C: One reason is that people no longer speak face-to-face or look at each other when having a conversation.

E: <u>Before, families used to have conversations at the dinner table, but now, people look down at their screens instead of across the table.</u>

Now You Try!

Distribute copies of "Before Smartphones" (page 135). Have students read the article and answer the questions on their Review & Practice handout, using the Before and After strategy to elaborate. Students may write their responses either on the handout or in their writer's notebook.

Note: You can differentiate this activity by having higher achievers ACE their whole response. For students who might be struggling with this concept, consider providing sentence starters or frames for E.

SAMPLE RESPONSES

1) According to the article "Before Smartphones," how did people make a phone call in the old days?

A: To make a call in the old days, people used a phone with a rotary dial.

C: According to the article, a caller had to put a finger through a numbered hole on the phone and turn the dial clockwise to a finger stop, then let go.

E: Before, a call went through after the person had finished dialing all the digits in the phone number. **Today,** callers can simply press a person's name in their contact list, or even just tell their phone to call the person.

2) Name one thing that's different between the phones your grandparents used and the phones we use today.

A: One thing that's different between the phones our grandparents used and the phones we use today is that today's phones are portable.

C: According to the article, in the old days people couldn't take their phones with them when they left the house.

E: Before, phones were heavy and had moving parts inside, so they had to stay wherever they were installed in the house. Today, phones are much smaller, lightweight, and portable, so people can carry them anywhere.

3) You are doing a science experiment on the three states of matter (solid, liquid, and gas). You put an ice cube in a plastic cup and then put the cup out in the sun for 20 minutes. What will happen to the ice cube in the cup?

A: The ice cube in the cup will turn into water.

C: Heat can melt some solids and turn them into liquid.

E: Before exposure to the sun, the ice would be in solid form, but after 20 minutes, the ice will melt and turn into the liquid form of water.

4) What is one of the most important events in women's history?

A: One of the most important events in women's history was gaining the right to vote.

C: In 1920, the 19th amendment was ratified, allowing women to vote.

E: Before the 1920s, women did not have the right to vote for their leaders, for their laws, or for their way of life. In today's society, equality in women's rights has significantly improved. Now, women can vote, have a voice, and can even become president.

5) What is one of the most life-changing events that happened in your life?

A: One of the biggest life-changing events for me was when my baby sister was born.

C: One reason is that there are now two kids in the family.

E: <u>Before she was born, I had no one else to play with except my parents. Now, I have a constant playmate who likes a lot of the same things I do, and we have so much fun together!</u>

Share and Reflect

Invite students to share their answers. Remind the class to listen for something interesting that one of their peers says. Then have them write a response using this frame.

- *I noticed _____ said _____.*
- *This made me think about _____.*

LESSON 9

USING THE "BEFORE AND AFTER" STRATEGY

Name: _____ Date: _____

TEACHING POINT

Critical thinkers can elaborate by using the "Before and After" strategy.

How Do I Do This?

1. Write down your A and C (your claim and evidence).

2. Push your thinking and ask yourself:

- What was the character like at the beginning of the book? What was the character like after _____ (event) in the book? What was the character like at the end of the book?
- What was life like before and after _____ (event)?
- What has changed since _____ (event) happened?
- How was life in _____ (period of history) compared to how life is now?

3. ACE your response using one of these sentence starters to elaborate.

- *Before . . . but after (or now) . . .*
- *In historical times . . . but in modern times . . .*
- *Historically . . . but in today's society . . .*
- *At the beginning . . . but by the end . . .*

Teacher Model
Bigger and Better

Q: How has television changed from when it first appeared?

A: Television has changed by becoming more accessible.

C: According to the article, every decade has brought vast improvements in television and people's ability to enjoy shows.

E: Before, "a fortunate few" viewed a show on a 2-by-3-inch, black-and-white screen, **but now,** with hundreds of channels available and high-definition TVs linked to the internet, people can watch anything they like anytime and anywhere.

Partner Practice

Work with your partner to practice the Before and After strategy. Read each question and the given A and C. Then use one of the sentence starters from Step 3 of How Do I Do This? to elaborate. If you or your partner is stuck, ask each other questions from Step 2.

1) Has technology improved our way of life?

A: Technology has improved our way of life.

C: One reason is that now we have access to so much information in the palm of our hand.

E: _____

_____

2) Has technology improved our way of life?

A: Technology has not improved our way of life.

C: One reason is that people no longer speak face-to-face or look at each other when having a conversation.

E: _____

_____

Now You Try!

Read "Before Smartphones" (from your teacher) and the questions below. Use the Before and After strategy to elaborate. Note that the A and C are already given, so use that information along with your own reasoning to fill in E.

1) According to the article "Before Smartphones," how did people make a phone call in the old days?

A: To make a call in the old days, people used a phone with a rotary dial.

C: According to the article, a caller had to put a finger through a numbered hole on the phone and turn the dial clockwise to a finger stop, then let go.

E: Before, _____

_____

Today, _____

_____

2) Name one thing that's different between the phones your grandparents used and the phones we use today.

A: One thing that's different between the phones our grandparents used and the phones we use today is that today's phones are portable.

C: According to the article, in the old days people couldn't take their phones with them when they left the house.

E: _____

_____

3) You are doing a science experiment on the three states of matter (solid, liquid, and gas). You put an ice cube in a plastic cup and then put the cup out in the sun for 20 minutes. What will happen to the ice cube in the cup?

A: The ice cube in the cup will turn into water.

C: Heat can melt some solids and turn them into liquid.

E: _____

_____

4) What is one of the most important events in women's history?

A: One of the most important events in women's history was gaining the right to vote.

C: In 1920, the 19th amendment was ratified, allowing women to vote.

E: _____

_____

5) What is one of the most life-changing events that happened in your life?

A: One of the biggest life-changing events for me was when my baby sister was born.

C: One reason is that there are now two kids in the family.

E: _____

_____

LESSON 10
Using the "Show Your Voice" Strategy

TEACHING POINT

Critical thinkers can elaborate by using the "Show Your Voice" strategy.

MATERIALS

- Review & Practice handout (pages 90–92)
- pink highlighters (optional)

Students will feel empowered with this lesson, knowing it's okay to use their own voice and opinion to elaborate upon evidence. The "Show Your Voice" strategy validates students' perspectives and helps them see that their opinions and personal experiences are all a valuable part of their schoolwork. This strategy is especially useful in persuasive or argumentative writing, debates, distinguishing opinion versus fact, and so on. When using this strategy, consider allowing students to use the first-person pronouns *I* and *my*, especially in informal essay writing, discussions, debates, or forums. With the goal of developing critical thinkers in mind, we should encourage students to practice developing an opinion, taking a stance on something, and expressing their thinking in an effective manner.

It would be a good idea to remind students of the difference between fact and opinion. When using the ACE strategy, C would be the place to present facts and E would be where they express their opinion about the topic.

Connect

Say to students: *Scholars, I've been so impressed with how you've been digging deeper into ways you can elaborate your claims. Depending on the topic or genre you are working on, sometimes it is appropriate to elaborate by voicing your personal opinion or your take on a certain topic. This is especially relevant when you're debating a topic or writing a persuasive or argumentative essay. You may certainly express your opinions or thoughts and show your own voice when ACE'ing a topic. Remember, the goal of elaborating effectively is not to repeat the evidence, but rather to make the evidence clear, relevant, and connected to the claim. Therefore, if you have a strong opinion about the A or C, you may state it in the E.*

Teach

Say to students: *Today we are going to learn another way to elaborate when ACE'ing a response. Today's strategy is called "Show Your Voice," and it means exactly what it says. When elaborating on a topic, oftentimes you can make your argument stronger when you add your own voice or perspective on the issue. Your voice and opinions are very valuable. Expressing them is another very effective way to elaborate your thinking. Let me show you an example so you know what I mean.*

A: Mrs. Smith is the best teacher in the school.

C: Because of her, my grades are now higher than they ever were.

E: In my opinion, if you have a teacher who can help raise your grades, that is one effective teacher!

Did you notice how I showed my voice about the C (the evidence)? Here's another example:

A: People should never text and drive at the same time.

C: According to DMV.org, texting while driving is one of the leading causes of death in teens.

E: From my perspective, pulling out a phone while driving just to type "LOL" to a friend's joke is not worth dying for.

HOW DO I DO THIS?

1. Write down your A and C (your claim and evidence).

2. Push your thinking and ask yourself:
   - *Do you agree or disagree with the topic? Why?*
   - *From your perspective, what do you think of the claim or evidence?*
   - *What's your opinion on the evidence?*

3. ACE your response using one of these sentence starters to elaborate.
   - *I (dis)agree with . . .*
   - *In my opinion . . .*
   - *I believe . . .*
   - *From my perspective . . .*

TEACHER MODEL

Let's take a look at an example about social media.

Q: Has social media improved our society?

A: Social media has not improved our society.

C: One reason is that some people have used it as a platform to hurt others.

E: In my opinion, the amount of pain a person can feel from social media is not worth the small benefits it can bring.

    Did you notice how I used the Show Your Voice strategy to show how my evidence supports my claim? Other elaboration sentences I could have used might include:

- **From my perspective,** there should be a way to penalize people who use social media to be hurtful or disruptive.
- **In my opinion,** misuse of social media should be treated like a punishable crime.

Partner Practice

Distribute copies of the Review & Practice handout. Then pair up students and say: *With your partner, look at each question and read the given A and C. Then try one of the Show Your Voice sentence starters to write the E. If you or your partner is stuck, prompt each other by asking questions from Step 2 in How Do I Do This?*

    Allow time for students to complete the activity. As they work, circulate around the room, keeping an eye out for outstanding examples of today's teaching point. Afterwards, invite students to share their responses with the class.

SAMPLE RESPONSES

1) Has social media improved our society?

A: Social media has not improved our society.

C: One reason is that social media seems to have taken away people's desire to talk to one another face-to-face.

E: <u>In my opinion, it is always better to actually communicate in person rather than on a screen.</u>

2) Has social media improved our society?

A: Social media has improved our society.

C: One reason is that people who have lost touch can connect with each other again.

E: <u>From my perspective, it is valuable for people to expand and grow their network of support. The more people you can be in touch with, the better.</u>

Now You Try!

Have students answer the questions on their Review & Practice handout, using the Show Your Voice strategy to elaborate. Students may write their responses either on the handout or in their writer's notebook.

Note: You can differentiate this activity by having higher achievers ACE the whole response. For students who might be struggling with this concept, consider providing the sentence starters or frames for E.

SAMPLE RESPONSES

(For 1 and 2): Should schools require students to wear uniforms?

1) A: No, schools should not require students to wear uniforms.

   C: One reason is that it takes away students' individuality and choice of style.

   E: <u>In my opinion, it's beautiful to see everyone come to school wearing different outfits, styles, and colors.</u>

2) A: Yes, schools should require students to wear uniforms.

   C: One reason is that it gives students one less thing to worry about.

   E: <u>From my perspective, students have enough pressure just trying to learn and maintain good grades. It would be great not to have to think about what to wear the next day.</u>

(For 3 and 4): Should animals be used for scientific testing?

3) A: Animals should never be used for scientific testing.

   C: One reason is that animal testing is cruel.

   E: <u>In my opinion, a life is a life, so animals should be treated with respect.</u>

4) A: Animals should be used for scientific testing.

   C: One reason is that animal testing can save lives.

   E: <u>In my opinion, a human's life is much more valuable than an animal's life. Therefore, if animals can be used to make medicine to save humans, it is worth it.</u>

(For 5 and 6): Which do you think is better—print books or e-books?

5) A: I think e-books are better than print books.

   C: One reason is that one small device can hold many books.

   E: <u>From my perspective, carrying one device that contains all my favorite books makes more sense than having to choose and carry only a few books when I go on vacation.</u>

6) A: I think print books are better than e-books.

   C: One reason is that people already spend too much time staring at their screens.

   E: <u>In my opinion, reading words on paper is much easier on the eyes. I also like the feel of flipping pages and seeing how far into a book I am.</u>

(For 7 and 8): Should students be allowed to use cell phones in class?

7) A: Students should be allowed to use cell phones in class.

   C: One reason is that phones can be useful learning tools.

   E: <u>From my perspective, if you can get information quickly at your fingertips, why not use it in a school setting?</u>

8) A: Students should not be allowed to use cell phones in class.

   C: One reason is that phones can be extremely distracting in class.

   E: <u>In my opinion, students will be too tempted to use their phones for reasons other than learning, so it is not worth it.</u>

Share and Reflect

Invite students to share their answers. Remind the class to listen for something interesting that one of their peers says. Then have them write a response using this frame.

- *I noticed _____ said _____.*
- *This made me think about _____.*

LESSON 10

USING THE "SHOW YOUR VOICE" STRATEGY

Name: _____ Date: _____

TEACHING POINT
Critical thinkers can elaborate by using the "Show Your Voice" strategy.

How Do I Do This?

1. Write down your A and C (your claim and evidence).

2. Push your thinking and ask yourself:
- Do you agree or disagree with the topic? Why?
- From your perspective, what do you think of the claim or evidence?
- What's your opinion on the evidence?

3. ACE your response using one of these sentence starters to elaborate.
- *I (dis)agree with . . .*
- *In my opinion . . .*
- *I believe . . .*
- *From my perspective . . .*

Teacher Model

Q: Has social media improved our society?

A: Social media has not improved our society.

C: One reason is that some people have used it as a platform to hurt others.

E: In my opinion, the amount of pain a person can feel from social media is not worth the small benefits it can bring.

Partner Practice

Work with your partner to practice the Show Your Voice strategy. Read each question and the given A and C. Then use one of the sentence starters from Step 3 of How Do I Do This? to elaborate. If you or your partner is stuck, prompt each other by asking questions from Step 2.

1) Has social media improved our society?

A: Social media has not improved our society.

C: One reason is that social media seems to have taken away people's desire to talk to one another face-to-face.

E: _____

_____

2) Has social media improved our society?

A: Social media has improved our society.

C: One reason is that people who have lost touch can connect with each other again.

E: _____

_____

Now You Try!

Use the Show Your Voice strategy to elaborate. Note that the A and C are already given, so use that information along with your own reasoning to fill in E.

(For 1 and 2): Should schools require students to wear uniforms?

1) A: No, schools should not require students to wear uniforms.

   C: One reason is that it takes away students' individuality and choice of style.

   E: _____

   _____

2) A: Yes, schools should require students to wear uniforms.

   C: One reason is that it gives students one less thing to worry about.

   E: _____

   _____

(For 3 and 4): Should animals be used for scientific testing?

3) A: Animals should never be used for scientific testing.

C: One reason is that animal testing is cruel.

E: _____

_____

4) A: Animals should be used for scientific testing.

C: One reason is that animal testing can save lives.

E: _____

_____

(For 5 and 6): Which do you think is better—print books or e-books?

5) A: I think e-books are better than print books.

C: One reason is that one small device can hold many books.

E: _____

_____

6) A: I think print books are better than e-books.

C: One reason is that people already spend too much time staring at their screens.

E: _____

_____

(For 7 and 8): Should students be allowed to use cell phones in class?

7) A: Students should be allowed to use cell phones in class.

C: One reason is that phones can be useful learning tools.

E: _____

_____

8) A: Students should not be allowed to use cell phones in class.

C: One reason is that phones can be extremely distracting in class.

E: _____

_____

ACE Short-Response Writing © Grace Long, Scholastic Inc.

LESSON 11
Using the "Say More" Strategy

TEACHING POINT
Critical thinkers can elaborate by using the "Say More" strategy.

MATERIALS

- Review & Practice handout (pages 98–100)
- "The Truth About Spiders" (page 135)
- pink highlighters (optional)

"Say More" is a simple strategy that many students probably already use without realizing it. As its name suggests, the Say More strategy simply says something more about the evidence or provides another piece of evidence related to the claim. Unlike the Explain Why strategy, in which students explain the significance of the evidence, this strategy simply expands on the evidence. This strategy is especially useful when writing an informational, argumentative, or persuasive response, as well as when giving scientific explanations.

At this point, students should be able to use multiple elaboration strategies in their ACE responses. Continue to review the name of each strategy, pointing it out to students as they use it: "Nice job using the Cause and Effect Strategy for your elaboration."

Connect

Say to students: *Thinkers, you've been doing an amazing job using various strategies to elaborate upon your thinking. Remember, always try to justify and elaborate your thinking without repeating or saying the same thing over and over again. The purpose of the C and E in ACE is to make your claim as clear as possible.*

Teach

Say to students: *Today we are going to learn another way to elaborate. Today's strategy is called "Say More." As its name implies, this new strategy is all about saying more—but without saying the same thing. Sometimes your elaboration just calls for you to explain more about the evidence you just provided. For example, if you're writing a report or providing factual information about something, sometimes you just need to give an additional fact or explain further what that fact really means. I will give you an example using a simple topic we've discussed before.*

A: Mrs. Smith is the best teacher in the school.

C: Because of her, my grades are now higher than they ever were.

E: For example, my grade point average is now 3.5. This makes it possible for me to apply to colleges I am interested in.

Notice that I simply "said more" about my evidence. I expanded upon it and by giving an example, I said more about it. Here's another example:

A: People should never text and drive at the same time.

C: According to DMV.org, texting while driving is one of the leading causes of death in teens.

E: When people are texting, their eyes, hands, and mind are not focused on traffic and other cars around them.

HOW DO I DO THIS?

1. Write down your A and C (your claim and evidence).

2. Push your thinking and ask yourself:
   - *Can you say more about your evidence?*
   - *Can you explain your evidence further or provide more definition?*
   - *Can you explain your evidence with another piece of evidence?*
   - *Can you explain your evidence by providing specific examples?*

3. ACE your response by using one of these sentence starters to elaborate.

- *Another way to look at (or say) it would be . . .*
- *In addition . . .*
- *To expand upon . . .*
- *For example . . .*
- *Furthermore . . .*
- *In fact . . .*

For this particular strategy, students probably don't need any of these sentence starters. Oftentimes, saying more comes naturally.

TEACHER MODEL

Display and read aloud the article "The Truth About Spiders" (page 135).

The Truth About Spiders

Q: Are spiders really as bad as many people think?

A: Spiders are not as bad as many people think.

C: According to the article, most spiders are harmless to humans.

E: In fact, spiders can actually be helpful to humans. Spider venom can be used to make medicines, and their silk may help scientists figure out new ways to make bridge parts.

Say to students: *Did you notice how I used the Say More strategy to support my* A? *We use this strategy to add more pieces of evidence to support our claim or to explain the evidence further.*

Partner Practice

Distribute copies of the Review & Practice handout. Then pair up students and say: *With your partner, look at each question and read the given A and C. Then try one of the Say More sentence starters to write the E. If you or your partner is stuck, prompt each other by asking questions from Step 2 in How Do I Do This?*

Allow time for students to complete the activity. As they work, circulate around the room, keeping an eye out for outstanding examples of today's teaching point. Afterwards, invite students to share their responses with the class.

SAMPLE RESPONSES

1) Has technology improved our way of life?

A: Technology has improved our way of life.

C: One reason is that now people can watch new movies without setting foot outside their house.

E: <u>For example, services such as Netflix, Hulu, or Amazon Prime allow people to watch any movie they'd like anytime it's convenient.</u>

2) Has technology improved our way of life?

A: Technology has not improved our way of life.

C: One reason is that people no longer speak face-to-face or look at each other when having a conversation.

E: <u>Because of this, misunderstandings often happen because feelings are sometimes misinterpreted over text or emails.</u>

Now You Try!

Have students answer the questions on their Review & Practice handout, using the Say More strategy to elaborate on their answers. Students may write their responses either on the handout or in their writer's notebook.

SAMPLE RESPONSES

(For 1 and 2): Which animal do you think makes a better pet—a cat or a dog?

1) A: I think a dog makes a better pet than a cat.

   C: One reason is that dogs are more playful than cats.

   E: For example, <u>people can go to the park with their dogs and play catch or run around. Not only do they have a lot of fun, both humans and dogs get plenty of exercise.</u>

2) A: I think a cat makes a better pet than a dog.

   C: One reason is that cats don't need someone to walk them.

   E: In fact, <u>cats simply go to their litter box to do their business. No need to take them out three times a day, rain or shine. All an owner has to do is clean up the litter box regularly.</u>

(For 3 and 4): Should kids get paid for doing chores?

3) **A:** Kids should get paid for doing chores.

   C: One reason is that it teaches them responsibility and the value of hard work.

   E: Kids are more likely to save money that they had to work hard for, instead of money that they received as a gift.

4) **A:** Kids should not get paid for doing chores.

   C: One reason is that parents do a lot of chores without getting paid.

   E: All family members should help with chores around the house because it's part of being a family unit. Working together brings the family together and gives kids a sense of belonging.

(For 5 and 6): What is one important aspect of democracy in the United States?

5) **A:** One important aspect of democracy in the United States is the right to vote.

   C: Any citizen 18 years or older has the right to vote in any election.

   E: Furthermore, this is regardless of race, gender, or socioeconomic status.

6) **A:** One important aspect of democracy in the United States is freedom of speech.

   C: The government cannot punish people for speaking their minds.

   E: There are some restrictions, of course, such as speaking obscenities, threatening violence, or sharing information that could harm national security.

Share and Reflect

Invite students to share their answers. Remind the class to listen for something interesting that one of their peers says. Then have them write a response using this frame.

- *When _____ (classmate) used the Say More strategy, I learned more about _____ .*

LESSON 11

USING THE "SAY MORE" STRATEGY

Name: _____ Date: _____

TEACHING POINT
Critical thinkers can elaborate by using the "Say More" strategy.

How Do I Do This?

1. Write down your A and C (your claim and evidence).

2. Push your thinking and ask yourself:
   - Can you say more about your evidence?
   - Can you explain your evidence further or provide more definition?
   - Can you explain your evidence with another piece of evidence?
   - Can you explain your evidence by providing specific examples?

3. ACE your response by using one of these sentence starters to elaborate.*
   - *Another way to look at* (or *say*) *it would be . . .*
   - *In addition . . .*
   - *To expand upon . . .*
   - *For example . . .*
   - *Furthermore . . .*
   - *In fact . . .*

Teacher Model

Q: Are spiders really as bad as many people think?

A: Spiders are not as bad as many people think.

C: According to the article, most spiders are harmless to humans.

E: In fact, spiders can actually be helpful to humans. Spider venom can be used to make medicines, and their silk may help scientists figure out new ways to make bridge parts.

* For this particular strategy, you may not even need any of these sentence starters. Oftentimes, saying more comes naturally.

Partner Practice

Work with your partner to practice the Say More strategy. Read each question and the given A and C. Then use one of the sentence starters from Step 3 of How Do I Do This? to elaborate. If you or your partner is stuck, prompt each other by asking questions from Step 2.

1) Has technology improved our way of life?

A: Technology has improved our way of life.

C: One reason is that now people can watch new movies without setting foot outside their house.

E: _____

_____

2) Has technology improved our way of life?

A: Technology has not improved our way of life.

C: One reason is that people no longer speak face-to-face or look at each other when having a conversation.

E: _____

_____

Now You Try!

Use the Say More strategy to elaborate. Note that the A and C are already given, so use that information along with your own reasoning to fill in E.

(For 1 and 2): Which animal do you think makes a better pet—a dog or a cat?

1) A: I think a dog makes a better pet than a cat.

C: One reason is that dogs are more playful than cats.

E: For example, _____

_____

2) A: I think a cat makes a better pet than a dog.

C: One reason is that cats don't need someone to walk them.

E: In fact, _____

_____

(For 3 and 4): Should kids get paid for doing chores?

3) A: Kids should get paid for doing chores.

C: One reason is that it teaches them responsibility and the value of hard work.

E: _____

_____

4) A: Kids should not get paid for doing chores.

C: One reason is that parents do a lot of chores without getting paid.

E: _____

_____

(For 5 and 6): What is one important aspect of democracy in the United States?

5) A: One important aspect of democracy in the United States is the right to vote.

C: Any citizen 18 years or older has the right to vote in any election.

E: _____

_____

6) A: One important aspect of democracy in the United States is freedom of speech.

C: The government cannot punish people for speaking their minds.

E: _____

_____

LESSON 12
Using the "Visualize It" Strategy

TEACHING POINT
Critical thinkers can elaborate by using the "Visualize It" strategy.

MATERIALS
- Review & Practice handout (pages 106–108)
- pink highlighters (optional)

The "Visualize It" elaboration strategy can be executed using any of these approaches: making mental images, sketching a picture, writing with details, or using pictures online. This strategy is applicable for writing or presenting persuasive topics, as well as for projects such as slideshow presentations and posters.

Connect

Say to students: *We've talked about various ways to show your thinking while you read. Today we are going to adapt one of our most helpful reading comprehension strategies as a way to elaborate. "Visualizing" is creating a mental or physical image of something to make a point. Have you ever been in a debate or an argument and said, "Imagine this . . ." or "Put yourself in my shoes . . ."? How many of you feel that when you have a picture of something, it helps you understand it better? This is a great way to get other people to see your point of view. This strategy is about justifying your claim by painting a picture in the reader's mind.*

Teach

Say to students: *When using the "Visualize It" strategy, you create a mental or actual image so the reader can better understand your claim. It's similar to when you're reading a book or an article and we ask you to visualize it to help you understand what's going on in the text. When you use the Visualize It strategy in your ACE response, you help your reader "see" a scenario, an example, or a situation. In a way you're trying to sway the reader's emotion with your elaboration to help justify your claim. Here is an example of using the Visualize It strategy with words:*

A: Mrs. Smith is the best teacher in the school.

C: One reason is that she takes the time to explain a concept to students if they didn't get it the first time.

E: Imagine this: You get a letter saying you might not graduate if you don't pass math class, but you have no one at home who can help you. So you ask your teacher for help, and she stays after school to help you understand the lesson and study for the exam. You get an A on the test, and now you can graduate.

If you're doing a presentation (instead of writing a response), you can provide images or a link to a video, for example, to prove your point.

HOW DO I DO THIS?

1. Write down your A and C (your claim and evidence).

2. Push your thinking by asking yourself:
   - *What do you want your readers to visualize? What do you want them to picture in their minds?*
   - *Is there a short story you can tell your readers that illustrates your evidence?*
   - *Is there an actual image you can provide?*

3. ACE your response using one of these sentence starters to elaborate. (If you are providing an actual image, insert the image and be sure to write a caption to explain.)
   - *Imagine . . .*
   - *Picture this . . .*
   - *Visualize . . .*
   - *This image/video/illustration shows . . .*

TEACHER MODEL

Let me show you a couple of different ways to use this strategy.

Q: Should students have homework after school?

A: Students should not have homework after school.

C: One reason is that kids need a break from all the thinking they've done at school during the day.

E: Picture this: You're a 7-year-old, and you've done your best to listen to your teacher all morning, working hard in reading, writing, math, and other subjects. You barely had time to play during recess or finish your sandwich during lunch. After a long afternoon filled with more work, you finally get to go home, only to open your folder to five more pages of homework you have to finish before going to bed!

Partner Practice

Distribute copies of the Review & Practice handout. Then pair up students and say: *With your partner, look at each question and read the given A and C. Then try one of the Visualize It sentence starters to write the E. If you or your partner is stuck, prompt each other by asking questions from Step 2 in How Do I Do This?*

Allow time for students to complete the activity. As they work, circulate around the room, keeping an eye out for outstanding examples of today's teaching point. Afterwards, invite students to share their responses with the class.

SAMPLE RESPONSES

1) Has technology improved our way of life?

A: Technology has improved our way of life.

C: One reason is that now people can watch new movies without setting foot outside their house.

E: Imagine it's been raining hard all day. You're in your pajamas drinking a nice warm cup of hot chocolate. You decide to have a spontaneous movie night with your family, and all you have to do is click on some buttons, and the movie appears right on your TV screen.

2) Has technology improved our way of life?

A: Technology has not improved our way of life.

C: One reason is that people no longer speak face-to-face or look at each other when having a conversation.

E: Visualize this . . . you want to show your parents the neat drawing you just finished. But instead they are on their phones, eyes glued to the screen, fingers texting away. They give you a quick glance, say, "How nice," and go right back to their texting!

Now You Try!

Have students answer the questions on their Review & Practice handout, using the Visualize It strategy to elaborate. Students may write their responses either on the handout or in their writer's notebook.

SAMPLE RESPONSES

1) Which animal do you think makes a better pet—a dog or a cat?

A: I think a dog makes a better pet than a cat.

C: One reason is that dogs are loyal to their owners.

E: Imagine you come home from a long, bad day at school. As soon as you walk in, a furry, cute, cuddly little puppy comes running up to you, wagging her tail as if you are the best thing that happened to her all day.

2) Should students have homework after school?

A: Students should not have homework after school.

C: One reason is that kids need to spend more time with their family.

E: Picture a 6th grader who goes to school from 8 AM to 3 PM, to soccer practice from 3 to 4, then to piano lessons from 4 to 5. When she gets home, she walks the dog from 5 to 5:30, eats dinner from 5:30 to 6, then does homework from 6 to 8. Then it's time to get ready for bed. When can she hang out with her family?

3) Should animal testing be banned?

A: Animal testing should not be banned.

C: One reason is that this research can save human lives.

E: Imagine you have a family member who was just diagnosed with a deadly disease, and there is a new drug that could potentially save your loved one's life. Wouldn't you want this drug to be tested to make sure it is safe and actually works?

4) Should kids get paid for doing chores?

A: Kids should get paid for doing chores.

C: One reason is that it teaches them responsibility and the value of hard work.

E: <u>Imagine people working at a restaurant—cooking meals, washing dishes, cleaning up, or serving customers their dinner. They get paid for their work, and kids should too.</u>

5) Should students have to wear uniforms in school?

A: Students should wear uniforms to school.

C: One reason is that you can still be unique and be yourself without having to think about what to wear to school.

E:

Share and Reflect

Invite students to share their answers. Remind the class to listen for something interesting hat one of their peers says. Then have them draw a quick sketch to reflect on what they heard.

LESSON 12

USING THE "VISUALIZE IT" STRATEGY

Name: _____ Date: _____

TEACHING POINT

Critical thinkers can elaborate by using the "Visualize It" strategy.

How Do I Do This?

1. Write down your A and C (your claim and evidence).

2. Push your thinking by asking yourself:

   - What do you want your readers to visualize? What do you want them to picture in their minds?

   - Is there a short story you can tell your readers that illustrates your evidence?

   - Is there an actual image you can provide?

3. ACE your response using one of these sentence starters to elaborate. (If you are providing an actual image, insert the image and be sure to write a caption to explain.)

   - *Imagine . . .*
   - *Picture this . . .*
   - *Visualize . . .*
   - *This image/video/illustration shows . . .*

Teacher Model

Q: Should students have homework after school?

A: Students should not have homework after school.

C: One reason is that kids need a break from all the thinking they've done at school during the day.

E: Picture this: You're a 7-year-old, and you've done your best to listen to your teacher all morning, working hard in reading, writing, math, and other subjects. You barely had time to play during recess or finish your sandwich during lunch. After a long afternoon filled with more work, you finally get to go home, only to open your folder to five more pages of homework you have to finish before going to bed!

Partner Practice

Work with your partner to practice the Visualize It strategy. Read each question and the given A and C. Then use one of the sentence starters from Step 3 of How Do I Do This? to elaborate. If you or your partner is stuck, ask each other questions from Step 2.

1) Has technology improved our way of life?

A: Technology has improved our way of life.

C: One reason is that now people can watch new movies without setting foot outside their house.

E: _____

_____

2) Has technology improved our way of life?

A: Technology has not improved our way of life.

C: One reason is that people no longer speak face-to-face or look at each other when having a conversation.

E: _____

_____

Now You Try!

Use the Visualize It strategy to elaborate. Note that the A and C are already given, so use that information along with your own reasoning to fill in E.

1) Which animal do you think makes a better pet—a dog or a cat?

A: I think a dog makes a better pet than a cat.

C: One reason is that dogs are loyal to their owners.

E: _____

_____

2) Should students have homework after school?

A: Students should not have homework after school.

C: One reason is that kids need to spend more time with their family.

E: _____

_____

3) Should animal testing be banned?

A: Animal testing should not be banned.

C: One reason is that this research can save human lives.

E: _____

_____

4) Should kids get paid for doing chores?

A: Kids should get paid for doing chores.

C: One reason is that it teaches them responsibility and the value of hard work.

E: _____

_____

5) Should students have to wear uniforms in school?

A: Students should wear uniforms to school.

C: One reason is that you can still be unique and be yourself without having to think about what to wear to school.

E:

Draw or glue a picture here.

PART III

Applying ACE to Paragraph Writing and State Testing

When we teach students new strategies, we want them to truly absorb the lessons and apply their newly learned skills inside and outside the classroom. This section shows students how to use ACE in writing paragraphs and on state assessments.

For many public school educators, state testing and other forms of standardized testing can be a sensitive or controversial topic. As teachers, we never want to "teach to the test." There are many valid reasons for this sentiment. Some teachers have a philosophy that does not support state testing at all. Some believe that state testing elicits undesired anxiety in both students and teachers. Others may be concerned about being judged based on their students' test scores.

This section is not about teaching to the test. Instead, the next few lessons are designed to show students how to apply what they've learned about ACE to the real world. We do not teach them what the answer is, but rather how to discover and explain the answer themselves. The goal of this next section is to provide explicit transference of skills and strategies and guide students to apply ACE in a variety of contexts.

At this point, students have been practicing the ACE strategy and should be comfortable with making a claim (A), citing evidence (C), and justifying their thinking through elaboration (E). The preceding lessons have taught them to be critical thinkers and provided them with cognitive skills and strategies to respond succinctly and effectively to questions. These next lessons will prepare them to utilize those skills more as they write longer paragraphs and take state assessments.

Test language can sometimes seem daunting, often making the questions seem harder than they really are or completely different from the context students are used to. These lessons support students through the reality of state assessments and give them a sense of "Oh, I know how to do this" or "I know what they're asking for." As students unlock the test for themselves, they should start to feel less anxious about it. With these explicit lessons, students will see clearly how they can use the ACE strategy in their assessments.

LESSON 13
ACE'ing Paragraphs

TEACHING POINT
Critical thinkers can use ACE(CS) to write eight-sentence paragraphs.

MATERIALS

- ACE Matrix (page 139)
- green, yellow, and pink highlighters for each student (or pair of students)
- Review & Practice handout (pages 114–115)

This lesson guides students to apply the ACE strategy to paragraph or essay writing. Eight-sentence paragraphs can be used to respond to any topic. Keep in mind that the paragraph does not necessarily have to be eight sentences; six is a good place to start, especially for lower grades. Using green (for A), yellow (C), and pink (E) highlighters will help you and your students identify components of the ACE structure that might be strong or lacking. For example, during a conference you might say, "I noticed you didn't highlight anything in pink. What elaboration strategy do you plan to use?"

To begin writing eight-sentence paragraphs with the ACE strategy, start with an accessible and applicable topic for most students. After students have written one cohesive paragraph, encourage them to use this structure for body paragraphs in argumentative or informational essays.

Connect

Say to students: *You've gotten very good at ACE'ing your responses. Now it's time to apply the ACE strategy to more than just three sentences. You're ready to turn it up a notch and expand your ACE responses into well-written eight-sentence paragraphs! You've probably heard of another similar concept of making a "paragraph sandwich." A sandwich has two slices of bread and all the good stuff in the middle. Similarly, an ACE paragraph has a topic sentence and concluding sentence (the bread) and all the evidence and elaboration in the middle.*

Teach

Say to students: *Today we will be writing paragraphs, so you will be doing more than just ACE. It will be more like "ACEs," or more specifically ACECECE(CS), in which your paragraph will have a few Cs and Es. The first sentence is your A—the claim. Next, you write a C to cite your evidence and an E to elaborate on that evidence, then another C and E, and another C and E. Finally, you wrap it up with a concluding sentence (CS).*

Display the ACE Matrix (page 139) on the board. Tell students: *This matrix lists sentence starters you can use for each of the ACE(CS) components. At first it might seem a little confusing, but it's just like following a pattern. Use the three highlighter colors to help you organize your thinking: green for your topic sentence (A), yellow for citing your evidence (C), and pink for your elaboration (E). Oftentimes, a little color can really help us as learners!*

HOW DO I DO THIS?

1. Make a claim. This is also known as your topic sentence.
   Highlight your topic sentence (A) in green.

2. Cite evidence—reasons and examples—to support your claim.
   Highlight your evidence (C) in yellow.

3. Elaborate on why your evidence is important.
   Highlight your elaboration (E) in pink.

4. Conclude with a statement that restates your claim.
   Highlight your concluding sentence (CS) in green.
   Sentence 1: A – *Topic sentence*
   Sentence 2: C – *Reason or example 1*
   Sentence 3: E – *Elaboration 1*
   Sentence 4: C – *Reason or example 2*
   Sentence 5: E – *Elaboration 2*
   Sentence 6: C – *Reason or example 3*
   Sentence 7: E – *Elaboration 3*
   Sentence 8: CS – *Concluding sentence*

Remind students: *Make sure your elaboration matches your evidence. For example, say my evidence in a criminal case is a bag of stolen goods found inside the suspect's car. I'm not going to say, "This shows that he's guilty because he likes ice cream." Although the criminal might indeed like ice cream, this fact does not support the evidence we are using.*

TEACHER MODEL

Display the following paragraph on the board. If possible, highlight the sentences using the correct color for each component. Emphasize sentence starters as you read this example.

> **(A)** Our classroom believes that teamwork is important for success. **(C) One reason** teamwork is important is that when we collaborate, we get a variety of ideas from other classmates. **(E) This is significant** because everybody has a different opinion or experience, so we must listen to one another. **(C) Another reason** teamwork is important is that we can accomplish more when we work together. **(E) If** two or more people work together on a project, **then** they can get the work done faster, saving everyone precious time. **(C) Another example** of why teamwork is important is that it can make us smarter. **(E) In our school experience,** there have been many times when one student struggled to understand a lesson but got help from a classmate. **(CS)** As you can see, teamwork has many benefits to everyone on the team.

Say: *Notice how this paragraph resembles a "sandwich" with green as your first and last sentences and yellows and pinks sandwiched in the middle.*

Partner Practice

Distribute copies of the Review & Practice handout. Then pair up students and say: *Here is a sample paragraph. Work with your partner to practice identifying the ACE(CS) components by using highlighters to color-code the ACE(CS) appropriately.*

Allow time for students to complete the activity. As they work, circulate around the room, keeping an eye out for outstanding examples of today's teaching point. Afterwards, invite students to share their responses with the class.

SAMPLE RESPONSE

(A) I think everyone should learn how to swim. **(C)** One reason is that knowing how to swim can save your life. **(E)** According to research, drowning is one of the most common causes of accidental death in children, and learning how to swim can help prevent such tragedies. **(C)** Another reason I think everyone should learn how to swim is that it's good exercise. **(E)** Swimming strengthens different muscles, such as your arms, legs, and core, and keeps your heart and lungs healthy. **(C)** Also, swimming is a lot of fun! **(E)** Imagine splashing around with your friends in the lake under the hot summer sun or playing Marco Polo in the pool. **(CS)** As you can see, it is quite evident that there are many benefits to learning how to swim.

Now You Try!

Challenge students to write an eight-sentence paragraph on a topic of their own choosing or using one of the prompts on their handout. Have them use highlighters to help them organize their sentences. Students may write their responses either on the handout or in their writer's notebook.

Share and Reflect

Invite students to share their eight-sentence ACE paragraphs. Tell the class: *Listen for something interesting that your peer has just said. Then write a response using this frame.*

- *I noticed _____ used the _____ elaboration strategy.*
- *This reminded me to _____.*

LESSON 13
ACE'ING PARAGRAPHS

Name: _____ Date: _____

TEACHING POINT
Critical thinkers can use ACE(CS) to write eight-sentence paragraphs.

How Do I Do This?

1. Make a claim. This is also known as your topic sentence.
   Highlight your topic sentence (A) in green.

2. Cite evidence—reasons and examples—to support your claim.
   Highlight your evidence (C) in yellow.

3. Elaborate on why your evidence is important.
   Highlight your elaboration (E) in pink.

4. Conclude with a statement that restates your claim.
   Highlight your concluding sentence (CS) in green.

> **Sentence 1: A** – Topic sentence
> **Sentence 2: C** – Reason or example 1
> **Sentence 3: E** – Elaboration 1
> **Sentence 4: C** – Reason or example 2
> **Sentence 5: E** – Elaboration 2
> **Sentence 6: C** – Reason or example 3
> **Sentence 7: E** – Elaboration 3
> **Sentence 8: CS** – Concluding sentence

Teacher Model

(A) Our classroom believes that teamwork is important for success. **(C) One reason** teamwork is important is that when we collaborate, we get a variety of ideas from other classmates. **(E) This is significant** because everybody has a different opinion or experience, so we must listen to one another. **(C) Another reason** teamwork is important is that we can accomplish more when we work together. **(E) If** two or more people work together on a project, **then** they can get the work done faster, saving everyone precious time. **(C) Another example** of why teamwork is important is that it can make us smarter. **(E) In our school experience,** there have been many times when one student struggled to understand a lesson, but got help from a classmate. **(CS)** As you can see, teamwork has many benefits to everyone on the team.

Partner Practice

Here is a sample paragraph. Use your highlighters to color-code the ACE(CS) appropriately. Work with a partner to help you.

> I think everyone should learn how to swim. One reason is that knowing how to swim can save your life. According to research, drowning is one of the most common causes of accidental death in children, and learning how to swim can help prevent such tragedies. Another reason I think everyone should learn how to swim is that it's good exercise. Swimming strengthens different muscles, such as your arms, legs, and core, and keeps your heart and lungs healthy. Also, swimming is a lot of fun! Imagine splashing around with your friends in the lake under the hot summer sun or playing Marco Polo in the pool. As you can see, it is quite evident that there are many benefits to learning how to swim.

Now You Try!

Choose one of the following prompts. Practice writing an eight-sentence paragraph using the ACE(CS) format. Don't forget to use your highlighters!

- Dogs make really great pets.
- Sharks are fascinating creatures.
- My mom (or dad) is the best.
- _____ is a good friend to me.

LESSON 14
Matching ACE With Test Terminology

TEACHING POINT
Critical thinkers can recognize and use the ACE strategy on standardized assessments.

MATERIALS

- Review & Practice handout (pages 120–123)
- ACE Test Buzzwords Table (page 144)
- scratch paper*
- "The Truth About Spiders" (page 135)
- "Mystery on the Beach" (page 136)
- "The Water Festival" (page 137)

This lesson will help students see that ACE is applicable in the "real world," especially in standardized assessments. When students have a comprehensive understanding of each component of Answer, Cite evidence, and Elaborate, they will be able to identify what the standardized test is asking them to do.

Connect

Say to students: *Thinkers, you've done a great job of ACE'ing your responses in reading, writing, and even math and science. You should*

---

* Most state assessments are now given electronically, which makes marking up the text (usually an effective comprehension strategy when students are provided hard copies of text) less practical—hence the use of scratch paper.

know that ACE is a strategy you can also use in other parts of your life. There will always be situations throughout your life in which you'll need to justify or defend your position on something. For example, when you apply for a job someday, you'll have to convince potential employers with evidence and elaboration as to why you're the best person for the job. Remember, the ACE strategy is not just about those three letters—it's about the thinking process that goes behind those letters. With this in mind, did you know that you can use ACE in standardized tests?

Teach

Say to students: *The purpose of standardized tests is to assess all the skills and standards you've been learning all year. This includes ACE. Believe it or not, you can use this strategy in a variety of ways on the tests. Although test makers might not use the letters A, C, and E or the words* Answer, Cite evidence, *or* Elaborate, *they use synonyms that mean the same thing. In class, we might call it* Answer, *but test makers might call it* inference or conclusion. *They might also ask questions in a way that you are not used to or in a different order. For example, they might give you the evidence from the text and ask you for the inference (A), or they might give you the conclusion and ask you to find text evidence (C). There are many words and phrases test makers might use that really mean* Answer, Cite evidence, *or* Elaborate.

Display the ACE Test Buzzwords Table (page 144) on the board and distribute copies to students. Say: *Take a look at this table.* Buzzwords *are words that are popular or fashionable at the moment. Test makers love to use buzzwords, but you should know these words are simply synonyms for components of ACE. We'll be referring to this ACE Buzzwords Test Table throughout this lesson.*

HOW DO I DO THIS?

1. Read the question carefully.

2. Do you see any of the test buzzwords?

3. Write "_____ = _____" on your scratch paper.

4. Determine what the question is giving you and what it is asking you to do.
   - *Is it giving you the A and asking you to find the C?*
   - *Is it giving you the C and asking you to find the A?*

5. Write it down: "They are asking for the _____."

TEACHER MODEL

Display and read aloud the short passage "The Truth About Spiders" (page 135). Then say: *Let's take a look at a sample test question.*

Example 1

Which sentence from the passage supports the idea that spiders can be helpful to humans?

(A) "Do you scream when you spot a spider?"

(B) "Most spiders have venom that is poisonous to insects but not to people."

(C) "You'll find out that spiders are fascinating!"

(D) "Things that spiders make, such as venom and silk, might come in handy for humans one day."

Say to students: *Can you see how this question is giving you the Answer ("the idea that spiders . . .") and is asking you to find the sentence that would support that claim (the evidence, or the C)? This is an example of a question that gives you the A and asks you to find the C. Let's look at the ACE Test Buzzwords Table. On my scratch paper, I would write: "Idea = A, Supports = C." I would then go back and reread the question to confirm that it has given me the A and is asking me to find the C. Then I would write on the scratch paper, "They are asking for the C." Of the answer choices, D gives the evidence that supports the idea that spiders can be helpful to humans.*

Let's take a look at more sample test questions.

Example 2

PART A: Which of these inferences about the author's purpose is supported by the text?

(A) The author describes people's reactions when they encounter spiders.

(B) The author explains that things spiders make can actually be beneficial to humans.

(C) The author explains that scientists are studying materials spiders use for webs.

(D) The author shows the importance of physical traits of spiders.

PART B: Which sentence from the text best supports your answer in Part A?

(A) "The truth is that most spiders are harmless to humans."

(B) "Scientists say that some of the chemicals in spiders' venom could be used to make new medicines for humans."

(C) "Many people are afraid of these eight-legged creatures."

(D) "Other scientists are studying spider silk, the superstrong, flexible material spiders use for webs."

In Part A, the question asks, "Which of these inferences . . .?" Refer to the ACE Test Buzzwords Table and write on scratch paper: "Inferences = Answer." Also write, "They are asking for the A." They are asking, What claim can you make after reading the passage? (Correct answer: B)

The Part B question asks, "Which sentence from the text best supports your answer in Part A?" Now that you have your A in ACE, what are they asking you to find in Part B? The question says "best supports." Write on scratch paper: "Supports = Cite evidence." They are asking for the C. (Correct answer: B) To make sure, I could write rewrite these test questions using the ACE strategy:

A: The author explains how things spiders make can actually be beneficial to humans.

C: According to the article, "Scientists say that some of the chemicals in spiders' venom could be used to make new medicines for humans."

E: (not being asked in this question)

Do the A and C match? Yes. This makes me believe I have both Parts A and B correct. Do you see how I'm using what I've learned about the ACE strategy and applying this skill to unlock what the test question is asking for?

Partner Practice

Distribute copies of the Review & Practice handout and "Mystery on the Beach" (page 136). Then pair up students and say: *Now I would like you and your partner to take a look at this sample test passage and questions. Follow the steps of How Do I Do This? to help you answer the questions. Remember, I want to see some thinking on your scratch paper to see if you can identify and match the test buzzwords with the ACE components.* Allow time for students to complete the activity.

SAMPLE RESPONSES

1. Supports = C, idea = A; asking for C (D)   **2. Part A:** inferences = A, supported = C; asking for A (A). **Part B:** supports = C; asking for C (C)

Now You Try!

Distribute copies of "The Water Festival" (page 137). Have students answer the questions on their Review & Practice handout to practice translating test buzzwords to matching components of ACE.

ANSWER KEY 1. B, D **2.** C **3.** C **4.** D **5.** Where the flooded lake's waters once spread, rice and vegetables will grow. This is also the time when the fishing season begins.

Share and Reflect

Invite students to share their answers. Remind them to listen for something interesting that one of their peers says. Then have them write a response using this frame.

• *Today I realized that _____ means the same thing as _____ in ACE.*

LESSON 14
MATCHING ACE WITH TEST TERMINOLOGY

Name: _____ Date: _____

TEACHING POINT
Critical thinkers can recognize and use the ACE strategy on standardized assessments.

How Do I Do This?

1. Read the question carefully.

2. Do you see any of the test buzzwords?

3. Write "_____ = _____" on your scratch paper.

4. Determine what the question is giving you and what it is asking you to do.

   • Is it giving you the A and asking you to find the C?

   • Is it giving you the C and asking you to find the A?

5. Write it down: "They are asking for the _____."

Teacher Model

Example 1

Which sentence from the passage <u>supports</u> the <u>idea</u> that spiders can be helpful to humans?

(A) "Do you scream when you spot a spider?"

(B) "Most spiders have venom that is poisonous to insects but not to people."

(C) "You'll find out that spiders are fascinating!"

(D) "Things that spiders make, such as venom and silk, might come in handy for humans one day."

On scratch paper, write: "Idea = A, Supports = C. They are asking for the C."

Example 2

PART A: Which of these <u>inferences</u> about the author's purpose is supported by the text?

(A) The author describes people's reactions when they encounter spiders.

(B) The author explains that things spiders make can actually be beneficial to humans.

(C) The author explains that scientists are studying materials spiders use for webs.

(D) The author shows the importance of physical traits of spiders.

PART B: Which sentence from the text best <u>supports</u> your answer in Part A?

(A) "The truth is that most spiders are harmless to humans."

(B) "Scientists say that some of the chemicals in spiders' venom could be used to make new medicines for humans."

(C) "Many people are afraid of these eight-legged creatures."

(D) "Other scientists are studying spider silk, the superstrong, flexible material spiders use for webs."

On scratch paper, write: "Inferences = A; Supports = C." Write out ACE to double check:

A: The author explains how things spiders make can actually be beneficial to humans.

C: According to the article, "Scientists say that some of the chemicals in spiders' venom could be used to make new medicines for humans."

E: (not being asked in this question)

Partner Practice

Work with your partner. Read "Mystery on the Beach" (from your teacher) and these sample test questions. Then follow the steps of How Do I Do This? and use your scratch paper to identify and match test buzzwords with the ACE components on test questions.

1) Which sentence from the passage supports the idea that female Kemp's ridley sea turtles do not wait for their babies to hatch?

(A) "How they get back is a mystery."

(B) "No one points the way or gives them directions."

(C) "Someday, the females will return to this beach."

(D) "Then, as soon as they lay their eggs, they return to the water."

2) PART A: Which of these inferences about Kemp's ridley turtles is supported by the text?

(A) The author explains that female Kemp's ridley turtles have an innate, natural sense of getting back to the gulf coast of Mexico to lay their eggs.

(B) The author describes how female Kemp's ridley turtles follow each other across the coast.

(C) The author explains that male Kemp's ridley turtles protect their eggs.

(D) The author describes how female Kemp's ridley turtles dig nests in the sand in order to protect their babies.

PART B: Which sentence from the text best supports your answer in Part A?

(A) "About eight weeks later, the baby turtles hatch."

(B) "The arrival of the Kemp's ridley turtles on this beach is called *arribada*."

(C) "All at once, all the turtles leave the water! It's as if they had received a silent underwater command to go ashore."

(D) "Under the cover of darkness, the babies find their way to the sea on their own."

Now You Try!

Read "The Water Festival" (from your teacher). Then answer the questions to practice translating test buzzwords to matching components of ACE.

1) PART A: What is most likely the author's intent by mentioning that the receding floodwaters leave behind mineral-rich soil ideal for farming?

(A) The author wants to inform how farmers utilize their natural resources.

(B) The author wants to explain why the Tonle Sap River is so valuable to Cambodians.

(C) The author wants to describe the cycle of farming at Phnom Penh.

(D) The author wants to convince readers that the Water Festival is the most celebrated holiday for Cambodians.

PART B: Which sentence from the text best illustrates the conclusion made in Part A?

(A) "The Water Festival celebrates the reversal of the river's life-giving waters."

(B) "The floodwaters expand the lake to many times its normal size."

(C) "On the last night, fireworks light up the skies over Phnom Penh."

(D) "Where the flooded lake's waters once spread, rice and vegetables will grow."

2) Which sentence from the text supports the claim that the Tonle Sap River is different from other rivers?

(A) "In the fall, the rains lessen."

(B) "For months, rain pours down almost every day."

(C) "The Mekong's powerful floodwaters push the Tonle Sap River backward!"

(D) "Tonle Sap Lake shrinks to its normal size."

3) Which sentence from the text supports the inference that the Water Festival ends in a similar fashion that Americans might end a celebration?

(A) "Exciting boat races are the main events of this unusual festival."

(B) "To watchers on the shore, the river looks like a moving stream of light."

(C) "On the last night, fireworks light up the skies over Phnom Penh."

(D) "For three days, hundreds of colorful boats will race along the Tonle Sap River."

4) "The boats are named after different farming groups and temples." This sentence supports the inference that _____.

(A) the Water Festival celebrates an amazing natural event

(B) more than 1,000 competitors participate in the Water Festival

(C) it is a beautiful sight to see a stream of lights floating down the river

(D) farmers and villagers are grateful for the fertile soil the floodwaters leave behind

5) Underline two sentences that best support the conclusion that the Tonle Sap River is an important resource for the Cambodian people.

Each fall, the receding floodwaters leave behind mineral-rich soil. Farmers depend on this soil to nourish their crops. Where the flooded lake's waters once spread, rice and vegetables will grow. This is also the time when the fishing season begins.

Every year, the entire cycle repeats. In the summer, the rains fall and Tonle Sap Lake floods. In the fall, the water recedes and the Tonle Sap River reverses its direction. And once again, the Water Festival celebrates the event with boat races.

LESSON 15
Using ACE in Standardized Tests

TEACHING POINT
Critical thinkers can ACE their written responses on standardized assessments.

MATERIALS

- Review & Practice handout (pages 129–130)
- ACE Test Buzzwords Table (page 144)
- "Kadimba's Field" (page 136)
- "The Story of the Three Little Pigs" (page 132)
- "Color Me Happy!" (page 138)
- computer (to practice typing in ACE response)
- scratch paper for practice

This lesson explicitly teaches students how to apply their ACE critical-thinking skills on standardized assessments. When students encounter open-ended questions or performance tasks related to informational or argumentative text, they should be able to confidently ACE their responses. The standardized assessment rubrics in writing state that in order to score a 4, students must show clear purpose, evidence and details, and effective elaboration in their writing.

Connect

Say to students: *Thinkers, we've talked about how critical thinkers like you can recognize ACE hidden in standardized assessments. We studied the ACE Test Buzzwords Table, which lists synonyms for the components of ACE (Answer, Cite evidence, and Elaborate). You've become experts in transferring your ACE strategy skills to show what you know. Today we will focus on how you can ACE your short-response answers on standardized tests. This is similar to what we do in social studies, math, language arts, and history, in which you respond to open-ended questions by writing a few sentences or a paragraph. As we discussed in the previous lesson, test makers may not explicitly say, "ACE this question," but this is what they want you to do. Remember when we learned how to ACE paragraphs in an informational or argumentative essay? Keep in mind that if you get this type of assignment on a performance task, they are asking you to ACE your response.*

Teach

Say to students: *In today's assessments, not all questions are multiple choice. We've discussed that the standards are always asking you to justify your answers, cite your evidence, and justify your thinking with elaboration. The state assessments will be asking you to do this as well. This is especially apparent when they ask open-ended questions and give you a box or space in which to write your response. Using the ACE strategy gives you a good place to start and helps you formulate your response.*

HOW DO I DO THIS?

1. Read the question carefully. Ask yourself: *Are they asking me to ACE my response here?*

2. Type or write out "A: C: E:" (each letter on its own line).

3. ACE your response:
   - **A** – *Make your claim by flipping the question.*
   - **C** – *Use details from the text as your evidence.*
   - **E** – *Elaborate on why your evidence supports your claim. (Choose which E strategy would be most applicable and jot down sentence starters that match that strategy.)*

4. Go back and delete "A: C: E:" and make any other edits so your response looks nice and clean.

Note: If you are using ACE in body paragraphs for a performance task, consider using scratch paper to ACECECE(CS) your response or to write out sentence starters to spark your thinking.

TEACHER MODEL

Some of you have gotten so good at ACE'ing that you may not even need to type out the letters "A: C: E:" but it certainly wouldn't hurt to do so. However, since test makers don't necessarily know the ACE strategy the way you do, if you type out "A: C: E:" make sure to go back and erase those letters and edit as necessary. Then you will have a nice, clean ACE response.

Let me show you what I mean. We'll use the story "Kadimba's Field" for practice. Display the story (page 136) on the board and read it aloud with the class.

> **Q: What can the reader infer about the main character's personality? Include information from the passage in your answer.**

Think aloud: *I noticed the word* infer, *which means the A. I need to provide an answer or claim about the character's personality. Then it says to include information from the passage. That signals C—cite evidence. Yes, I need to ACE this response. I'm going to set up my response this way.* (You may want to type up the response below and display it on the board for students to see.)

> **A:** The reader can infer that the main character is very clever.
>
> **C:** In the story, Kadimba devised a plan for the elephant and the hippo to do all the work for him so his field would be ready for planting.
>
> **E:** Most people would have either done it themselves or never gotten the work done, but Kadimba found another way to solve his problem.

Did you see how I used "Flip It" for the A? Did you see how I referred to the text for my C? And did you notice which E strategy I use? I used Compare and Contrast. So this is how I would type my answer to help me organize my ACE response. Then I would go back and delete the "A: C: E:" since the test makers probably don't know what that is. (Note: It's unlikely that points would be taken off for leaving the letters in the response, but it might be worth mentioning, just in case.) *So my final response will look like this:*

> The reader can infer that the main character is very clever. In the story, Kadimba devised a plan for the elephant and the hippo to do all the work for him so his field would be ready for planting. Most people would have either done it themselves or never gotten the work done, but Kadimba found another way to solve his problem.

Did you see how I ACE'd my response? When a test asks you to use details from the text to support your answer, that is a signal to use the ACE strategy that you know so well.

Partner Practice

Distribute copies of the Review & Practice handout. Pair up students and say: *With your partner, practice thinking like a test maker. Brainstorm some questions that would require you to use ACE for your response. This will help you review the components and practice your ACE thinking skills, instead of just focusing on the acronym. Use the ACE Test Buzzwords Table to help you.*

Allow time for students to complete the activity. As they work, circulate around the room, keeping an eye out for outstanding examples of today's teaching point. Afterwards, invite students to share their responses with the class.

SAMPLE RESPONSES

- What is the theme of the text? Use details from the text to support your answer.
- What is the author's purpose in using the phrase "_____" in the sentence below?

Now You Try!

Distribute copies of "Kadimba's Field" (page 136), "The Story of the Three Little Pigs" (page 132), and "Color Me Happy" (page 138). Have students use them to answer the questions on their Review & Practice handout. The purpose of this activity is for students to recognize that the questions are asking them to ACE their response and to set up their papers so they have the structure right in front of them. In a sense, they are making their own scaffold to support their thinking.

To give students additional practice, you may want to design your own questions or find sample test items online or from your own class. The next step would be to have students write out their ACE responses for practice test questions.

SAMPLE RESPONSES

1) Read "The Story of the Three Little Pigs" and "Kadimba's Field." In what ways are the third little pig and Kadimba similar? Provide two pieces of <u>evidence</u> from different sources that <u>support this claim</u> and <u>explain how each example supports</u> this claim.

Evidence = C   Support this claim = A   Explain = E

Notice how ACE is out of order? That's okay. This question is certainly asking for an ACECECE(CS) paragraph response, so here's one way students can set up their paper:

A:

C:

E:

C:

E:

CS:

2) Parents are buying a new crib for the baby. They need to make sure the parts fit into the car. The car can fit an object that is 15 feet long. The crib has two parts. The first part is 10 feet long, and the second part is 3 feet long. Will the crib parts fit into the car? Explain your answer.

A: Yes/No, the crib parts will/will not fit into the car.

C: According to my calculations of . . . (Show calculations and drawings.)

E: (Use elaboration strategy "Explain Why" and/or "Cause and Effect.")
This shows that . . .
If . . . then . . .

3) Read the passage "Color Me Happy!" Your teacher just asked you to choose the color for your classroom walls. What color would you choose? Justify your answer and support it with information from the source.

A:
C:
E:
C:
E:
CS:

Share and Reflect

Have students write a response using this frame.

* *The most helpful strategy I used today was _____ because _____.*

LESSON 15
USING ACE IN STANDARDIZED TESTS

Name: _____ Date: _____

TEACHING POINT
Critical thinkers can ACE their written response on standardized assessments.

How Do I Do This?

1. Read the question carefully. Ask yourself: *Are they asking me to ACE my response here?*

2. Type or write out "A: C: E:" (each letter in its own line).

3. ACE your response:

- **A** – Make your claim by flipping the question.
- **C** – Use details from the text as your evidence.
- **E** – Elaborate on why your evidence supports your claim. (Choose which E strategy would be most applicable and jot down sentence starters that match that strategy.)

4. Go back and delete "A: C: E:" and make any other edits so your response looks nice and clean.

Note: If you are using ACE in body paragraphs for a performance task, consider using scratch paper to ACECECE(CS) your response or to write out sentence starters to spark your thinking.

Teacher Model

Q: What can the reader infer about the main character's personality? Include information from the passage in your answer.

A: The reader can **infer** that the character is very clever.

C: In the story, Kadimba devised a plan for the elephant and the hippo to do all the work for him so his field would be ready for planting.

E: Most people would have either done it themselves or never gotten the work done, but Kadimba found another way to solve his problem.

> The reader can infer that the character is very clever. In the story, Kadimba devised a plan for the elephant and the hippo to do all the work for him so his field would be ready for planting. Most people would have either done it themselves or never gotten the work done, but Kadimba found another way to solve his problem.

Partner Practice

With your partner, practice thinking like a test maker. Brainstorm some questions that would require you to use ACE for your response. Use the ACE Test Buzzwords Table (from Lesson 14) to help you.

_____

_____

_____

_____

_____

Now You Try!

Analyze the following test question examples. How could you apply the ACE strategy to each question? Set up your scratch paper or computer screen accordingly.

1) **Read "The Story of the Three Little Pigs" and "Kadimba's Field." In what ways are the third little pig and Kadimba similar? Provide two pieces of <u>evidence</u> from different sources that <u>support this claim</u> and <u>explain how each example supports</u> this claim.**

2) **Parents are buying a new crib for the baby. They need to make sure the parts fit into the car. The car can fit an object that is 15 feet long. The crib has two parts. The first part is 10 feet long, and the second part is 3 feet long. Will the crib parts fit into the car? Explain your answer.**

3) **Read the passage "Color Me Happy!" Your teacher just asked you to choose the color for your classroom walls. What color would you choose? Justify your answer and support it with information from the source.**

APPENDIX
Text Passages, Charts, and Templates

This section includes text passages that accompany some of the lessons in this book, plus reference charts to support your teaching.

Text Passages (pages 132–138) Provide students with their own copy of each text. Whether using hard copies or electronic copies, students benefit from practicing close reading skills and marking up the text, which often leads to deeper comprehension. Deeper understanding of content will inevitably elicit more critical thinking in students' ACE responses.

ACE Matrix (page 139) This comprehensive resource provides sentence starters for each component of ACE. The columns are organized by genre or types of context ACE assignments might be given in the classroom. Refer to this resource when creating your own assignments and lessons that require an ACE response.

Elaboration Matrix (pages 140–141) This chart is designed to support the heart of the ACE strategy, which is elaboration. Encourage students to name the elaboration strategy they are using and practice asking the appropriate questions to elicit thoughtful responses.

Elaboration Poster (page 142) This reproducible mini-poster provides students with various sentence starters for each elaboration strategy. Have students put a copy in their writer's notebook for easy reference.

ACE 8-Sentence Paragraph Template (page 143) Use this graphic organizer as a supplement to Lesson 13: ACE'ing Paragraphs. You might consider writing a few sentence starters in the boxes before making copies for the class.

ACE Test Buzzwords Table (page 144) This table serves as an "ACE synonyms chart" and can be very helpful when teaching students how to unpack test questions.

The Story of the Three Little Pigs

Once upon a time, there lived an old mother pig and her three little pigs. When the little pigs were old enough, they moved out.

The first little pig was very lazy. He didn't want to work at all, so he quickly built his house out of straw. The second little pig was also lazy, but he worked a bit harder than the first one. He built his house out of sticks. Then, the two little pigs sang and danced and played together the rest of the day.

The third little pig didn't join them. He worked hard all day, building his house with bricks. It was a well-made house with a nice fireplace and chimney. Even the strongest of winds could not blow it down.

The next day, a wolf was walking by the road where the three little pigs lived. He saw the straw house and smelled the pig inside. He thought the pig would make a tasty meal. So the wolf knocked on the door and said:

"Little pig! Little pig! Let me in!"

But the first little pig saw the wolf's big paws through the peephole. He answered back:

"Uh-uh! Not by the hairs on my chinny chin chin!"

The wolf replied:

"Then I'll huff and I'll puff and I'll blow your house down."

So he huffed, and he puffed, and he blew the house down! The first little pig scurried away to hide with the second little pig.

The wolf followed him to the house made of sticks. He smelled the pigs inside. He thought they would make a delicious dinner. So the wolf knocked on the door and said:

"Little pigs! Little pigs! Let me in!"

But the two little pigs saw the wolf's pointy ears through the peephole. They answered back:

"Uh-uh! Not by the hairs on our chinny chin chin!"

The wolf replied:

"Then I'll huff and I'll puff and I'll blow your house down."

So he huffed, and he puffed, and he blew the house down! The two little pigs scampered away to hide with the third little pig.

The wolf chased them and almost caught them. They made it inside the brick house just in time and slammed the door shut. Now the wolf could smell all three pigs inside. He knew they would make a scrumptious feast. So the wolf knocked on the door and said:

"Little pigs! Little pigs! Let me in!"

But the three little pigs saw the wolf's narrow eyes through the peephole. They answered back:

"Uh-uh! Not by the hairs on our chinny chin chin!"

The wolf replied:

"Then I'll huff and I'll puff and I'll blow your house down."

So he huffed, and he puffed. And he puffed, and he huffed. Then he huffed and huffed, and he puffed and puffed. But he could not blow the house down. The wolf was so out of breath that he couldn't huff and puff anymore.

He stopped to rest under the tree next to the house. That's when he saw the chimney. As the wolf climbed up to the roof and balanced across the ridgepole, the third little pig built a blazing fire and put on a big pot of water to boil. When he heard the wolf coming down the chimney, the third little pig pulled off the lid. *Plop!* Into the scalding water the wolf fell.

And that was the end of the big bad wolf!

Too Plugged In

In today's world, screens are nearly everywhere. Computers and smartphones connect us with friends or help us do research for school projects. In fact, some health experts say watching TV or playing video games can be relaxing.

But many kids spend a lot more time on these devices than they should. On average, American kids spend about seven hours a day in front of screens. The American Academy of Pediatrics (AAP) is a leading group of doctors. It says that all that extra screen time could lead to problems like weight gain, lower grades in school, and trouble sleeping.

SCREEN OVERDOSE

David Greenfield is an expert on how people use technology. He says that time spent playing video games is time not spent being active.

"If you spend 8, 9, 10 hours a day gaming, the only thing you're moving is your finger," says Greenfield.

Being surrounded by screens can also make it hard to focus on one task. In a 2013 study, experts in California studied students as they did their homework. After just two minutes, many kids started surfing the internet, watching TV, or texting instead of focusing on their assignments.

Too much screen time at night can also cause kids to lose out on sleep. Studies have shown that playing video games or using other digital devices right before bedtime can keep kids tossing and turning all night. The light from the screen tricks the brain into thinking it's still daytime.

POWERING DOWN

The AAP says kids should limit their screen time to no more than two hours a day. One way kids can limit their screen time is by taking plenty of screen breaks during the day. Kids could use those breaks to rest their brains or exercise.

The Dove and the Ant

A gray dove and a red ant lived peaceably in the same part of a forest. Though they hardly knew each other, they lived as pleasant neighbors.

One morning, the ant went to the riverbank for his morning drink. The river was running faster and higher than normal because of heavy rains the night before. Alas, the ant tumbled into the river and was carried along its rushing current. The dove happened to be sitting in a tree beside the river. When she noticed the ant's unhappy accident, she took pity on him. So she plucked a small branch from the tree and dropped it into the river. The ant then grabbed onto the branch and used it as a boat to return to shore.

Later that morning, the ant noticed a sly hunter in the shadows of the forest. He was aiming his bow toward the tree where the dove was resting. Without hesitation, the ant immediately stung the hunter sharply on his foot. This made him jump in surprise and pain, so he couldn't let his arrow fly.

This is how a tiny ant saved the life of a gentle dove.

Two Hands on the Paddle

It was a warm, sunny morning when Uncle Sid took Brenda and Brandon to kayak on Walden Pond. They carried a three-person kayak, paddles, and safety vests to the beach and prepared for their voyage. It was early, so their kayak was the first one to launch.

Uncle Sid showed the kids how to paddle and talked about safety. Then he helped Brenda into the front cockpit and lowered Brandon into the middle one. Uncle Sid took the rear cockpit, and they headed out.

Brenda wanted to take photos, but Uncle Sid warned, "Two hands on the paddle." Uncle Sid first paddled alone as the children watched. Then they joined in. The ride was choppy at first, but once the three found a rhythm, the kayak moved smoothly.

They headed for Ice Fort Cove—Uncle Sid's favorite spot. It was there that Brandon tumbled out of the kayak! He was pointing at a fish leaping out of the water. In his excitement, Brandon dropped his paddle overboard and tried to grab it. But he lost his balance and took a surprise dip in the pond! Uncle Sid snatched his soaked nephew at once and lifted him back into the kayak.

"Glad it's warm today," he chuckled.

Bigger and Better

Back in 1927, Americans got their first peek at television. On this electronic wonder with its 2-inch-by-3-inch, black-and-white screen, a fortunate few watched a speech given by Herbert Hoover.

A decade later, people could watch on slightly larger sets, some with 9-inch screens (measured diagonally). They watched in astonishment. But television was still in its infancy. Very few families owned a set.

After World War II, TV sales skyrocketed; about 1 in 200 families nationwide had one. That number leaped to more than 9 in 10 households by the 1960s, when TV screens got much larger. Then, with the arrival of color, fascination increased again. Yet, there were very few channels people could watch.

With the coming of cable in the 1970s, the number of channels multiplied. Then, in the 1980s, TV viewing itself changed with the invention of devices that let people record programs and then watch them whenever they wished. Next, in the late 1990s, high-definition televisions changed the game again. These HDTVs displayed clearer, sharper pictures on even larger, flat-panel screens. Today, with further improvements in technology, TVs are linked to computers and the internet.

What's next for TV?

Before Smartphones

Telephones had already made the world smaller when your grandparents chatted on them. People used phones to talk to friends on the next block, in the next town, even in another country. Like today's smartphones, Grandma's phone provided convenient communication at any time.

When she was a girl, Grandma probably used a rotary phone. Connected by wires to central switching stations, this kind of phone had a heavy base that sat on a table. Its handset, bulky and as long as a hero sandwich, held both the receiver for listening and the transmitter for speaking. Yet there was nothing to press to make a call. Rather, Grandma dialed each digit of a phone number by poking her finger into a numbered hole, turning the dial clockwise to the finger stop, and letting go. After all digits were dialed, the call went through.

Many homes had just one rotary phone that a family shared. Compact but heavy, with moving parts inside, the phone stayed put. You didn't take it with you; you used the phone wherever it had been installed.

Those dinosaurs are barely recognizable today. Compared with them, digital smartphones are sleek, lightweight, multipurpose, and portable. One-piece smartphones have touch screens rather than round dials. Unlike rotary phones, wireless smartphones can take messages, send e-mails, access the internet, play music, snap photos, and let you play games. And yes, they make and receive calls, too.

The Truth About Spiders

Do you scream when you spot a spider? If so, you're not alone! Many people are afraid of these eight-legged creatures. But scientists say that very few spiders are dangerous.

"The truth is that most spiders are harmless to humans," says Rod Crawford, a spider expert in Seattle, Washington. In fact, he and other experts say that spiders actually help people. Things that spiders make, such as venom and silk, might come in handy for humans one day.

Most spiders have venom that is poisonous to insects but not to people. Scientists say that some of the chemicals in spiders' venom could be used to make new medicines for humans.

Other scientists are studying spider silk, the superstrong, flexible material spiders use for webs. They hope to copy it to make things such as parts for bridges.

So what should you do the next time you see a spider building a web? "Spend some time watching it," says Crawford. "You'll find out that spiders are fascinating!"

Mystery on the Beach

One night in Mexico, on a beach lit only by moonlight, a baby is born. In the dark, the baby leaves the beach. She travels hundreds, maybe thousands, of miles away. Fifty years later, she returns to the same place where she was born.

Who is this mysterious female? She is a giant Kemp's ridley sea turtle.

Kemp's ridley turtles feed in the waters all along the coastline of North America. During the summer months, many swim as far north as Long Island, New York, to munch on crabs and other local seafood. But at nesting time, female Kemp's ridley turtles all head for the same place—the beach on the gulf coast of Mexico where they were born. How they get back is a mystery. They have no map. No one points the way or gives them directions. Yet they never get lost.

The arrival of the Kemp's ridley turtles on this beach is called *arribada* (*arribada* means "arrival" in Spanish). It's an unbelievable show! All at once, all the turtles leave the water! It's as if they had received a silent underwater command to go ashore. The turtles dig nests in the sand. Then, as soon as they lay their eggs, they return to the water.

About eight weeks later, the baby turtles hatch. Under the cover of darkness, the babies find their way to the sea on their own. Someday, the females will return to this beach. How will they know when and where to go? That is the mystery!

Kadimba's Field
BANTU FOLKTALE

Clever Kadimba was a lazy hare. It was time to plant crops to feed his family, but he hated to work. Tangled bushes throughout his field made the job daunting. Even after clearing the field, Kadimba would still have to dig rows for his crops.

Kadimba hatched a plan. He dragged a thick rope across his field. Then he waited by one end for Elephant to appear. Kadimba dared Elephant to a tug-of-war. The tusker roared but agreed. He twisted his trunk around the rope. Kadimba said, "When you feel my pull, then pull back." He raced to the opposite side of the tangled field and rested by the other end of the rope. Elephant waited patiently.

Soon Hippo waddled by. Kadimba offered this giant the same challenge. Hippo agreed, letting the hare wrap the rope 'round his muddy body. Kadimba said, "When you feel my pull, then pull back." Hippo waited good-naturedly.

Kadimba then dashed to the middle of the rope and tugged in each direction. Feeling the pull, Elephant and Hippo began tugging. They yanked, grunted, and heaved in astonishment. They pulled back and forth, left and right, struggling until nightfall. By then, the rope had torn out all the tangled bushes; the thrashing had softened the soil. Kadimba's field was ready for planting.

The Water Festival

Up go 50 oars! Down come 50 oars! Fifty rowers give a powerful thrust. The boat surges forward as the race begins! Thousands of people cheer their favorite boats.

It is November. More than 1,000 competitors from all over Cambodia have gathered at the nation's capital, Phnom Penh. Today is the first day of the annual Water Festival! For three days, hundreds of colorful boats will race along the Tonle Sap River.

BACKWARD-FLOWING RIVER

The Water Festival celebrates an amazing natural event. Normally, the Tonle Sap River flows from Tonle Sap Lake into the Mekong River. Each summer, though, the monsoon rains come. For months, rain pours down almost every day. The Mekong River fills with raging waters. The Mekong's powerful floodwaters push the Tonle Sap River backward! Instead of flowing into the Mekong, it flows into the lake! Then, this lake—the largest in Southeast Asia—becomes even larger. The floodwaters expand the lake to many times its normal size.

In the fall, the rains lessen. The dry season begins. The water level goes down. Then the Tonle Sap River reverses its direction. Once again, it flows from the lake into the Mekong River. Tonle Sap Lake shrinks to its normal size.

TIME TO CELEBRATE

The Water Festival celebrates the reversal of the river's life-giving waters. Exciting boat races are the main events of this unusual festival. The boats are named after different farming groups and temples. On the last night, fireworks light up the skies over Phnom Penh. This signals the festival's end. Then boats hung with lighted lanterns float down the river. To watchers on the shore, the river looks like a moving stream of light.

LIFE-GIVING WATERS

Each fall, the receding floodwaters leave behind mineral-rich soil. Farmers depend on this soil to nourish their crops. Where the flooded lake's waters once spread, rice and vegetables will grow. This is also the time when the fishing season begins.

Every year, the entire cycle repeats. In the summer, the rains fall and Tonle Sap Lake floods. In the fall, the water recedes and the Tonle Sap River reverses its direction. And once again, the Water Festival celebrates the event with boat races.

Color Me Happy!

Do you like blue candy? Most people avoid blue food, because most foods are not naturally blue. Our brains just don't connect the color blue with tasty food. Try this: Replace the bulb in your refrigerator with a blue bulb. When you look at blue milk and eggs, you'll probably stop feeling hungry!

However, blue could have a different effect as a room color. In one classroom that had dark blue walls, students got significantly higher test scores. In dark blue gyms, weight lifters lifted heavier weights.

How can this effect be explained? Scientists think that color may affect your mood. And the way you feel influences the way you behave.

In a dark blue room, students might feel strong and smart. If the walls are pale blue, students may not pay attention. Yellow walls could make students nervous—and jumpy students don't do well on tests!

So, if you want to feel happy, strong, and smart, think about the colors surrounding you. Changing colors can change your mood.

ACE Matrix

Genre	General, Conversational	Fiction, Literary Response	Nonfiction, Expository, Content Areas	Argumentative, Persuasive, Justification
ANSWER	• I believe . . . • I think . . . • In my opinion . . . • From my perspective . . .	• ___ can be considered . . . • The theme of the story is . . . • The character's personality can be described as . . .	• ___ is/is not . . . • ___ can be considered . . . • ___ is better than . . . • ___ can be explained by . . . • The answer to ___ is . . . • The solution to ___ is . . . • One way to support my thinking is . . .	• After much research, I strongly believe . . . • After thoughtful consideration, I firmly believe . . . • People should/should not . . .
CITE EVIDENCE	• One reason . . . • For example . . . • Another reason . . . • From my experience . . .	• For example . . . • On page ___, the character said/did/acted/reacted/felt/was treated . . . • On page ___, paragraph ___, the text states . . .	• One piece of evidence would be . . . • In paragraph ___, the text states . . . • According to the author . . . • One example would be . . . • One way to solve the problem would be . . . • One way I can support my thinking is . . .	• One significant fact is . . . • According to the article . . . • One reason I hold this position . . . • From personal experience . . . • There is a story about . . . • One example is . . . • According to statistics . . .
ELABORATION	**Explain Why** • This shows that . . . • This is significant because . . . **Show Your Voice** • In my opinion . . . • From my perspective . . . . **Compare and Contrast** • Most ___, but	**Explain Why** • This is significant because . . . • This shows that . . . **Author's Purpose** • The author's purpose in ___ was . . . • Perhaps the author's reason for ___ was . . . **Show Your Voice** • In my opinion . . . **Real-World Connection** • This is similar to . . . • In the real world . . . **Compare and Contrast** • Most ___, but . . . • ___ could have ___, but instead . . .	**Explain Why** • This is significant because . . . **Cause and Effect** • Due to ___ . . . • This is caused by . . . • One effect of ___ is . . . . **Author's Purpose** • The author's purpose in ___ was . . . • Perhaps the author's reason for ___ was . . . **Before and After** • Before . . . but after (or now) . . . • In historical times . . . but in modern times . . . • Historically . . . but in today's society . . .	**Explain Why** • This proves that . . . • This is significant because . . . **Show Your Voice** • In my opinion . . . • From my perspective . . . **Visualize It** • Imagine . . . • Picture this . . . • Visualize . . . • (Show an image or share a link)
CONCLUSION SENTENCES	• As you can see . . . • It is evident that . . .	• In conclusion . . . • To summarize . . .	• It is clear that . . . • The evidence indicates . . .	• It is clear that . . . • The evidence indicates . . .

Elaboration Matrix

Elaboration Strategy	Especially Applicable Genres and Content Areas	Questions to Prompt Thinking	Possible Sentence Starters	Example ACE Response
EXPLAIN WHY	All content areas	• Why is this important? • Why would this matter to the reader? • How does this prove that your evidence is related to your claim? • As a lawyer, how could you convince the jury that your evidence is important?	• This shows that . . . • This is significant because . . . • As you can see . . .	**A:** I would describe the third little pig as smart. **C:** In the story, it states that he built his house with bricks. **E:** This shows that he was thoughtful and wise about what material he used to build his house. He knew that if he built his house with bricks, it would be sturdy and couldn't be blown away.
CAUSE AND EFFECT	All, science, math	• What are the effects of this issue? • What are the consequences of ___? • If this happens, then what?	• One effect of ___ is . . . • If ___, then . . . . • Due to ___, . . . • One impact ___ might/would . . .	**A:** Children should have limits on their screen time. **C:** According to the article, American kids spend an average of seven hours a day looking at their screens. **E:** One effect of kids spending that much time looking at their screens is that the kids don't get enough physical exercise.
COMPARE AND CONTRAST	Argumentative, explanatory, informational, persuasive, social studies, literary analysis	• How is ___ the same as or different from other ___? • What does ___ do that's different from what others do? • What's the opposite of ___? • What makes ___ unique or different from others?	• Most ___, but . . . • Unlike ___, . . . • ___ could have ___, but instead . . .	**A:** I would describe the third little pig as smart. **C:** In the story, it states that he built his house with bricks. **E:** Unlike the other two little pigs, the third little pig put some thought into what material would last.
REAL-WORLD CONNEC-TION	All content areas	• Does this ___ remind you of another ___? • Has there been an issue or topic that you've heard of somewhere (for example, in the news) that can help explain your claim? • Can you think of an analogy to explain your point?	• This is similar to . . . • This reminds me of . . . • In the real world, this is like . . . • A similar scenario would be . . .	**A:** I would describe the third little pig as smart. **C:** In the story, it states that he worked hard all day to build his house with bricks. **E:** This reminds me of the ancient Egyptians, who took 20 years to build the Great Pyramid. It still stands today, even after thousands of years.

BEFORE AND AFTER	All, science, history, literary response	• What was the character like at the beginning of the book? What was the character like after ___ (event) in the book? What was the character like at the end of the book? • What was life like before and after ___ (event)? • What has changed since ___ (event) happened? • How was life in ___ (period of history) compared to how life is now?	• Before . . . but after (or now) . . . • In historical times . . . but in modern times . . . • Historically . . . but in today's society . . . • At the beginning . . . but by the end . . .	**A:** Television has changed by becoming more accessible. **C:** According to the article, every decade has brought vast improvements in television and people's ability to enjoy shows. **E:** Before, "a fortunate few" viewed a show on a 2-by-3-inch, black-and-white screen, but now, with hundreds of channels available and high-definition TVs linked to the internet, people can watch anything they like anytime and anywhere.
SHOW YOUR VOICE	Classroom debate, persuasive, history, science	• Do you agree or disagree with the topic? Why? • From your perspective, what do you think of the claim or evidence? • What's your opinion on the evidence?	• I (dis)agree with . . . • In my opinion . . . . • I believe . . . • From my perspective . . .	**A:** Social media has not improved our society. **C:** One reason is that some people have used it as a platform to hurt others. **E:** In my opinion, the amount of pain a person can feel from social media is not worth the small benefits it can bring.
SAY MORE	Informational, explanatory, science, math	• Can you say more about your evidence? • Can you explain your evidence further or provide more definition? • Can you explain your evidence with another piece of evidence? • Can you explain your evidence by providing specific examples?	• Another way to look at (or say) it would be . . . . • In addition . . . . • To expand upon . . . . • For example . . . . • Furthermore . . . . • In fact	**A:** Spiders are not as bad as many people think. **C:** According to the article, most spiders are harmless to humans. **E:** In fact, spiders can actually be helpful to humans. Spider venom can be used to make medicines, and their silk may help scientists figure out new ways to make bridge parts.
VISUALIZE IT	All, oral presentations, persuasive, descriptive writing, argumentative	• What do you want your readers to visualize? What do you want them to picture in their minds? • Is there a short story you can tell your readers that illustrates your evidence? • Is there an actual image you can provide?	• Imagine . . . • Picture this . . . . • Visualize . . . . • This image/video/illustration shows . . .	**A:** Students should not have homework after school. **C:** One reason is that kids need a break from all the thinking they've done at school during the day. **E:** Picture this: You're a 7-year-old, and you've done your best to listen to your teacher all morning, working hard in reading, writing, math, and other subjects. You barely had time to play during recess or finish your sandwich during lunch. After a long afternoon filled with more work, you finally get to go home, only to open your folder to five more pages of homework you have to finish before going to bed!

ELABORATION POSTER

Explain Why

- This shows that . . .
- This is significant because . . .
- As you can see . . .

Before and After

- Before . . . but after (or now) . . .
- In historical times . . . but in modern times . . .
- Historically . . . but in today's society . . .
- At the beginning . . . but by the end . . .

Cause and Effect

- One effect of ___ is . . .
- If ___, then . . .
- Due to . . .
- One impact ___ might/would . . .

Show Your Voice

- I (dis)agree with . . .
- In my opinion . . .
- I believe . . .
- From my perspective . . .

Compare and Contrast

- Most ___, but . . .
- Unlike ___, . . .
- ___ could have ___, but instead . . .

Say More

- Another way to look at (or say) it would be . . .
- In addition . . .
- To expand upon . . .
- For example . . .
- Furthermore . . .
- In fact . . .

Real-World Connection

- This is similar to . . .
- This reminds me of . . .
- In the real world, this is like . . .
- A similar scenario would be . . .

Visualize It

- Imagine . . .
- Picture this . . .
- Visualize . . .
- This image/video/illustration shows . . .

ACE 8-SENTENCE PARAGRAPH TEMPLATE

Name: _____ Date: _____

A Answer the question	
C Cite evidence	
E Elaborate	
C Cite evidence	
E Elaborate	
C Cite evidence	
E Elaborate	
CS Concluding sentence	

ACE TEST BUZZWORDS TABLE

IN CLASS, WE SAY:	Answer	Cite evidence	Elaborate	ACE paragraph, 8-sentence paragraph
ON THE TEST, THEY SAY:	• Inference • Conclusion • Claim • Summarize the central idea • Main idea • Central idea • Opinion • Suggested • Author's purpose • What is most likely true?	• Best illustrates • Supports • Justify • Evidence • Detail • Facts • Include information from the passage • Give examples	• Justify • Elaborate • Explain how each example supports the claim	• Body paragraph • Short answer • Short response